Portraits: Friends and Strangers

PORTRAITS

Friends and Strangers

MICHAEL MATHERS

Madrona Publishers, Inc.   *Seattle*

Library of Congress Cataloging In Publication Data

Mathers, Michael H
    Portraits: friends and strangers.

    1. Photography—Portraits. 2. Mathers,
Michael H.   I. Title.
TR680.M365   779'.2'0924   79-336
ISBN 0-914842-36-6
ISBN 0-914842-35-8 pbk.

Madrona Publishers, Inc., 2116 Western Avenue, Seattle, WA 98121

TO MY MOTHER AND FATHER

With special thanks to Raymond and Gretel

FOREWORD

"I was one of the curious," Michael Mathers writes, explaining how he came to be in the home of an elderly woman who was reading auras. "Curious," however, just doesn't do him justice, this self-described "visual dog in heat" whose hunger impels him into a Skid Row hotel, has him stepping over a pile of eight-inch rubber penises, draws him to a slaughterhouse, a funeral home, a drag queen ball. Takes him to Fossil, Oregon. And leads him over and again to the homes of his friends. "As is my nature," he writes, "I brought my camera."

Powerful individually, as a collection these portraits overwhelm. If at first we are sure which people are "straight," which not, soon we are lost. Who, really, are the gargoyles here? About to look out through the window at the "stupid bastards" who pay to stare at her, the carnival's Fat Lady is sure she knows who the real freaks are.

Were these portraits only a record of the grotesque, they would arrest attention, but they compel a far more subtle view. Mathers catches the strangeness of us all, yet seldom passes judgment. These are our lives, he seems to be saying; we all have to learn to live with ourselves, whatever others take us to be. See us as. With an eye for the rich and strange in even the familiar, Mathers gives us a Chaucerian world. No blemishes removed; nothing expurgated; nothing denied. One wonders how they—we—took such forms. See the child in his father's arms. No one immune. Yet in this collection there is little despair; like it or not, this is God's plenty. Faced with such accumulation, what can one do but nod in recognition?

The elderly woman who was reading auras told Mathers that she saw a black spot over his heart. "That got to me," he writes. "I knew what she was talking about. I'd come there because . . . it sounded a bit bizarre and I had hoped to get it on film." It's true, it's true, this photographer intrudes, he's a driven man, but how he pays his dues! There are no candids in this collection: over and again Mathers had to ask if he could *make* a picture. Not *take* it. What he takes are chances, exposing not merely film but himself to such strange flowerings.

He returns to the aura reader, he writes, "just to talk." Well, not really. On his final visit she poses for a portrait. She made the right choice.

The last photograph in this collection is, of course, of the artist. Who is this naked but masked man? I think we look for him best in the extraordinary pages that go before, a cumulative self-portrait of a man who, unblinking, has embraced life on its own terms.

THOMAS FARBER

Portraits: Friends and Strangers

Illili

If you're ever in San Francisco you should stay at the El Drisco Hotel. It's relatively inexpensive ($28 for two), but old-world and majestic. On top of Pacific Heights overlooking the bay, each room is furnished with antiques. Original paintings hang on the walls. Staying there is a visual pleasure, but don't expect much from the restaurant and be willing to wait at least five minutes for outgoing calls. The hotel is never crowded—there are nine permanent residents and the rest of the rooms are often vacant. The hotel's motto, found on matchbook covers and stationery letterheads, reads, "Never a life lost to fire."

In one of the El Drisco's rooms I did this picture of Illili, a mischievous elf of a man who, a few years before, had made millions at Columbia Records as the agent for Sly and the Family Stone and other groups. The pace and atmosphere finally got to him. He quit and became a Sufi. Now he travels around the country entertaining kids with songs, skits and laughter—performing at grade schools and hospitals, usually for free. He wants to be remembered for bringing joy and laughter into people's lives.

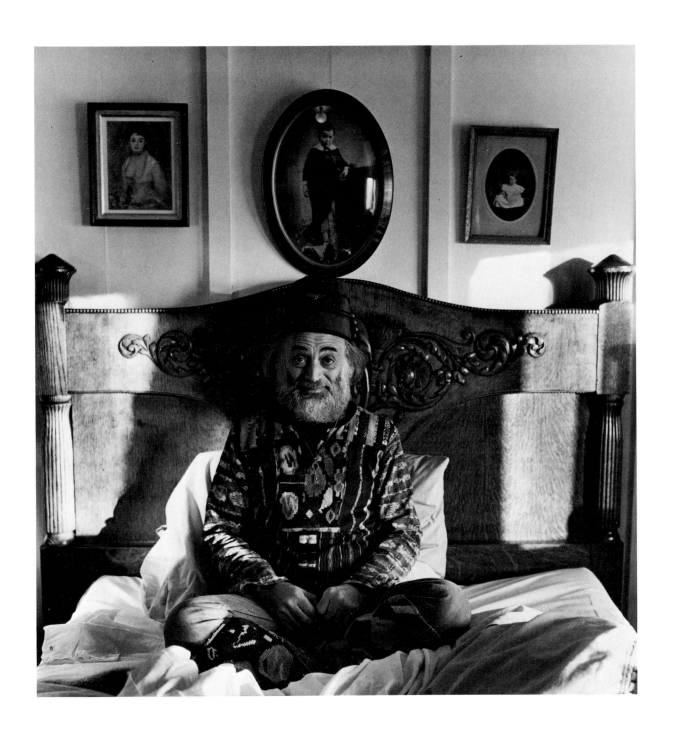

Helen Hall

Driving along a four-lane highway in Florida, I passed this woman and had to stop and talk. I learned she had been walking around the country promoting good will between citizens and police. At night the local cops would put her up in an empty cell. She had been doing this for twelve years.

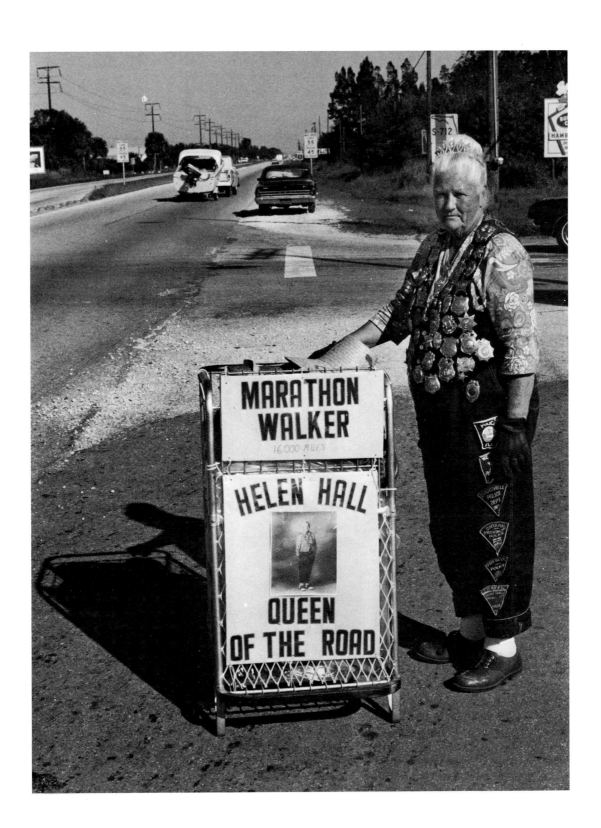

Boy Scout Leader

On a hot August afternoon a rally was being held at the city's coliseum for President Ford. I was under the impression it would be a political gathering for all ages with placards, ''America, love it or leave it'' buttons, straw hats with red, white and blue bands. But as it turned out the participants were all children: Brownies, Girl Scouts, Cub Scouts, Boy Scouts and a few Eagle Scouts. Hundreds of them, carrying American flags. They were having a great time horsing around while they waited for the doors to open. A handful of adults were there to supervise and maintain some semblance of order—keep them in line, prevent fights, console those in tears and return stolen hats. This scoutmaster was one of those grown-ups.

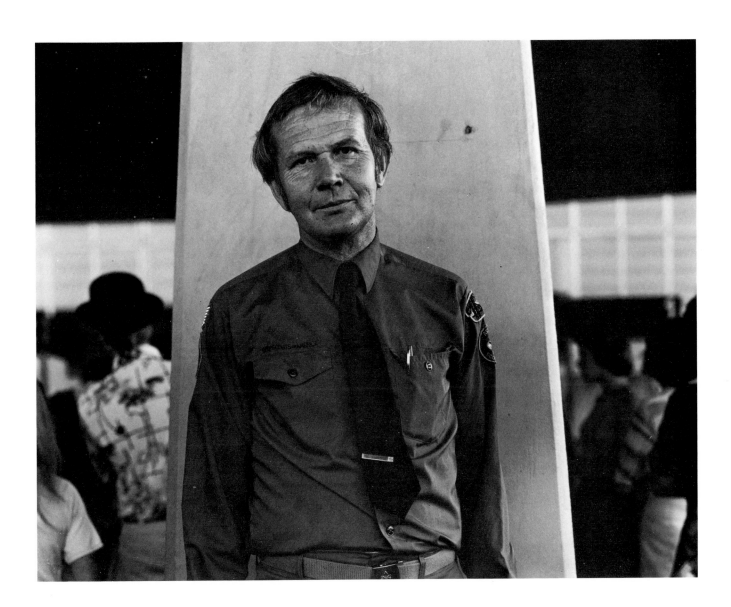

Hearse Driver

I visited several funeral parlors asking to do portraits but in each case was politely refused. I guess they were still smarting from Jessica Mitford's book *The American Way of Death*. Undaunted, I went to the Chapel of Roses, a modest-size funeral home with an especially large parking lot. The front room consisted of a receptionist's alcove, a sofa and a small pool with a scantily clad figurine in the center spouting a fine spray of water. Artificial lilies floated at her feet. I talked with the owner, who was cordial but did not want any pictures taken in the place. He was glad to give me a guided tour, though. We started in the display room, which housed a dozen coffins of varying prices, passed through the tastefully decorated waiting or mourning rooms, and went into the chapel. The size of a small church, the chapel was dimly lit around the pews but well lit at the altar. An open coffin surrounded by flowers was next to the pulpit. We walked up the aisle. The coffin was occupied by an old man, ashen-faced, wearing a black suit. After a few polite remarks the owner and I went outside to view the hearses. It was there he suggested that I do a portrait of one of his drivers.

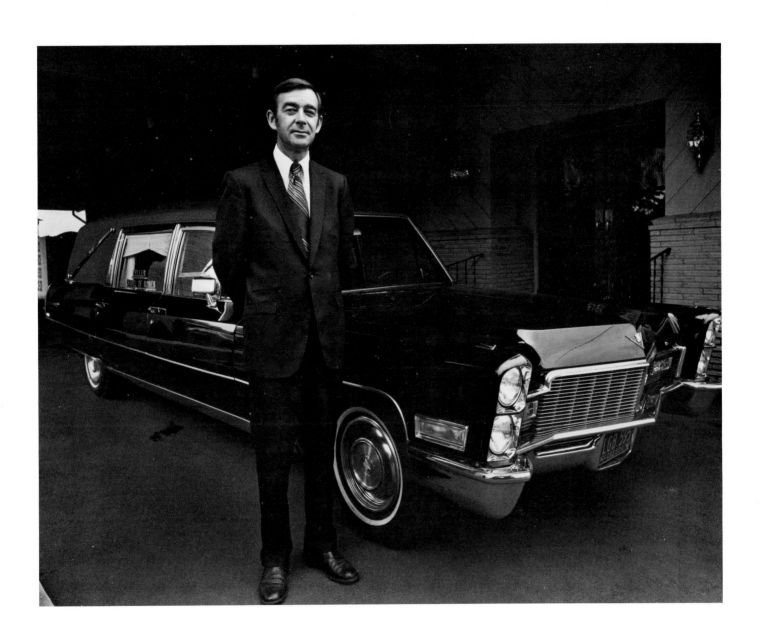

Sara

    She was at a museum opening in Santa Fe when I first saw her. Immediately struck by her vivaciousness and courtly bearing, I was a visual dog in heat. I wanted to do a portrait but was afraid to ask. Later, at a party, with enough alcohol in me, I had the courage. She accepted and the following day I drove to Taos where she lived and was about to open a gallery. The session lasted an hour, but I never felt I captured her spirit. As I was packing up my gear, she stood against the wall talking with me; I saw this picture and knew it was the one.

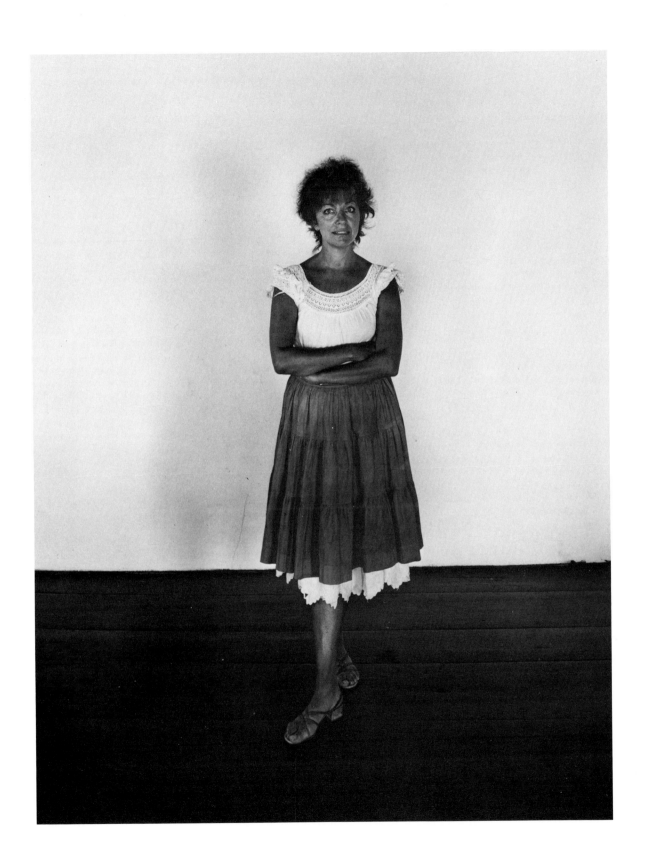

Blaine

A friend and photographer. A natty dresser, he reminds me of a twenties artist living in Paris. This was his studio—he only likes doing his own work and won't accept any commercial jobs. At the time of this picture he was photographing during the day and working nights as a janitor in a department store.

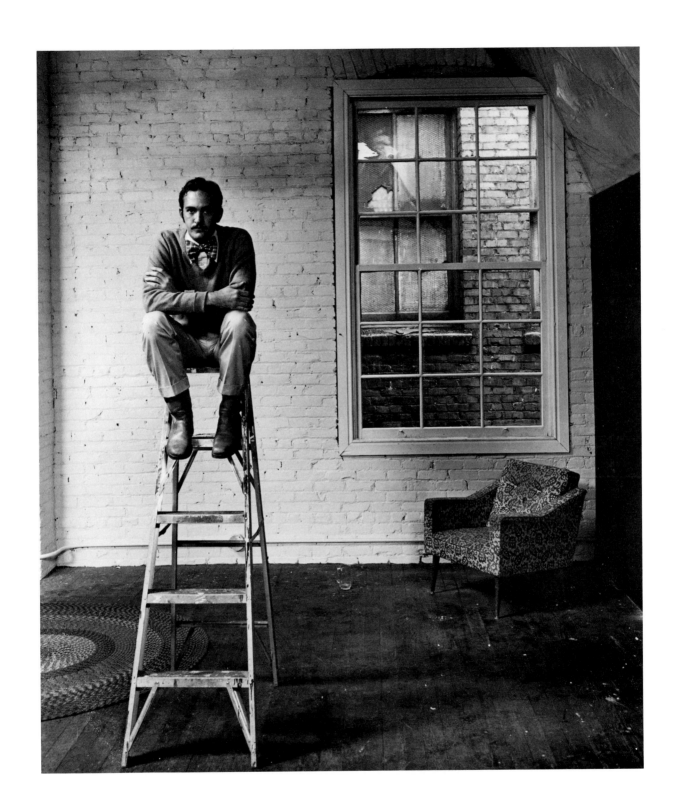

Glorious Swanson

She's a she when in drag and a he when he's not. He's forty-two and is a successful management analyst. For years he has been fascinated by Gloria Swanson and has collected every bit of printed and pictorial material he can find on her. He's seen every one of her movies many times, especially *Sunset Boulevard*, from which he can recite all of her lines. Prompted by some friends who were queens to try drag, he did it as a joke one night several years ago and, naturally, chose Gloria. Since then he's studied her every pose. He's especially fond of her over-the-hill, arrogant gestures.

When Gloria Swanson went to Portland a couple of years ago, she was met at the airport by Glorious. In his scrapbook he has a letter from her commenting on how much she appreciated her reception and how elegant Glorious looked.

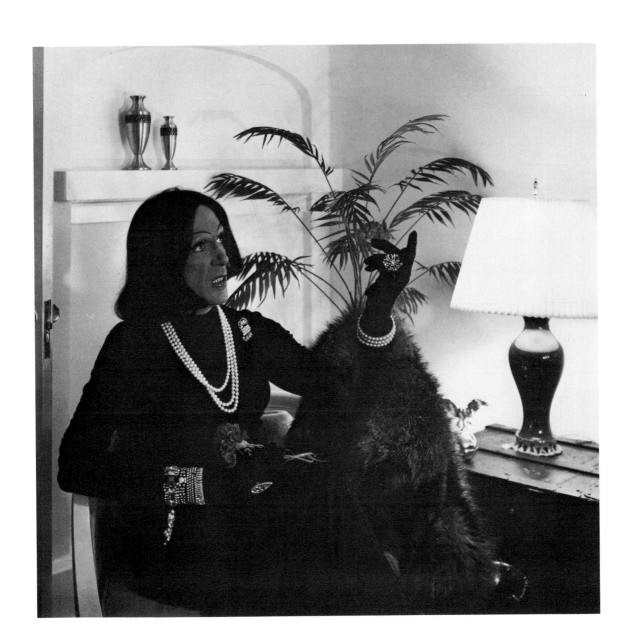

Gynecologist

Bob is now a good friend, but that was not the case when I made this portrait. I saw him then as an arrogant, sexist doctor, insensitive to his patients, perhaps even a misogynist. All these feelings were confirmed when I went to his office for the photo session. It was my first visit to a gynecologist's examination room. It looked like a twentieth-century torture chamber, and Bob was the torturer. I wanted to show all this in a picture—I wanted to nail him, and I did. Now, however, knowing him better, I would make a very different portrait because I discovered he's a dedicated man who is a doctor not for the money or the prestige, but because he wants to be of service.

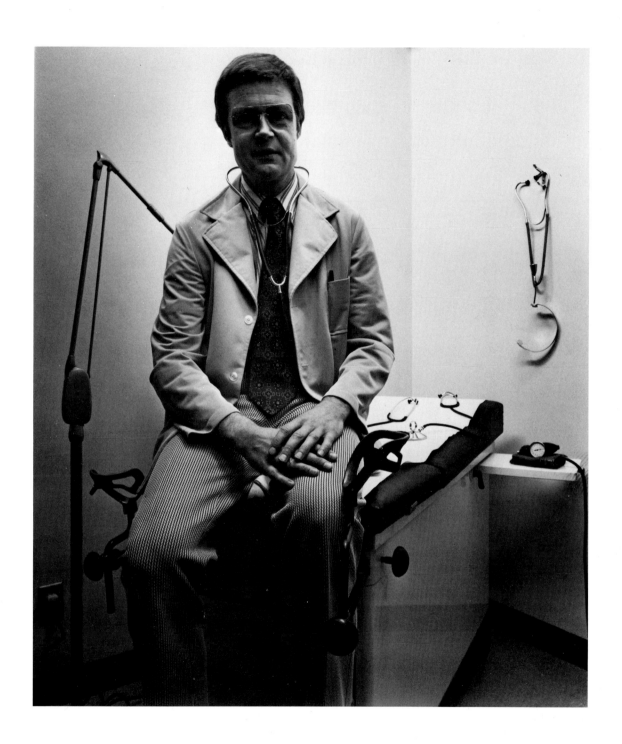

Rocky

Twenty-four and of gypsy descent, he's never learned to read or write. He makes his living buying and selling elegant but used clothing. He scours second-hand stores and estate sales. Occasionally he makes his own clothes for special occasions. This was one of his costumes.

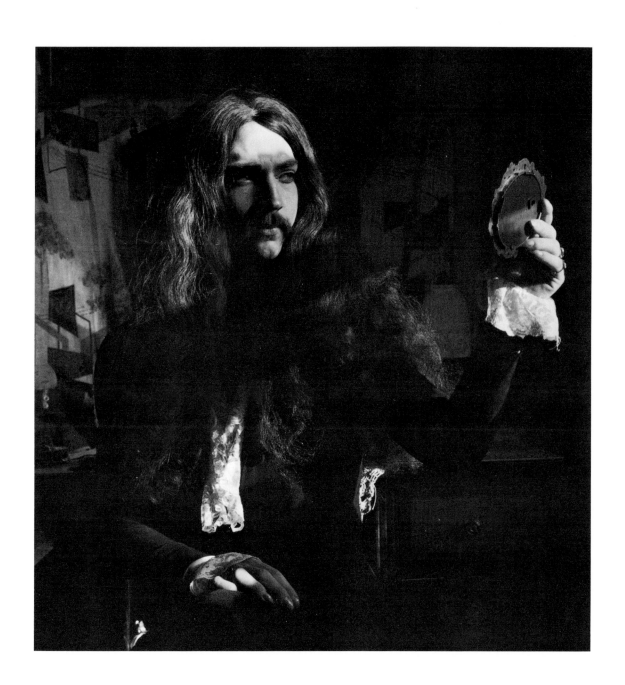

My Cousin Marion

A cousin several times removed. I met her at a family
party and her beauty and energy astounded me. She
works in New York as an actress.

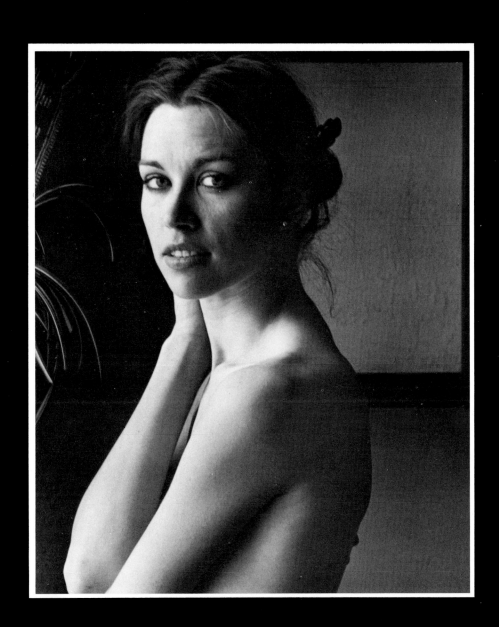

Buckaroo

His name is Ashley Aiken. He's a shy, majestic kind of man. He'd worked for years as a cowboy, and I was told by someone on the ranch that he had been a Hollywood stunt man in his youth but never liked to talk about it.

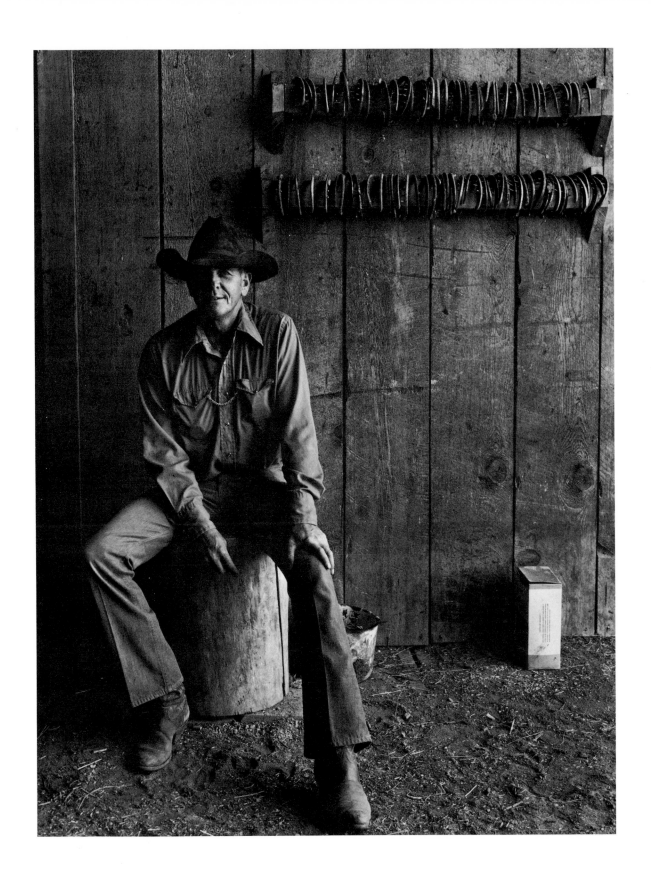

Cello Maker

Gretel, a friend, and I were collaborating on a book about people dedicated to their work. We stopped in a small sleepy town in Iowa because years before she had worked there on a film in which one of the characters was a magician and escape artist. We went to the police station to track him down and perhaps find other likely candidates. We spent an amusing thirty minutes discussing our problem with one of the policemen. He gave us the magician's name and address plus two others. One was a professor at the local college who had invented a space language for communicating with anyone or anything that happened to land here from outer space. The other was this cello maker, who had lived in Cleveland for years teaching English. His hobby was making cellos. He tired of the academic life, moved to Iowa and turned his hobby into a paying profession.

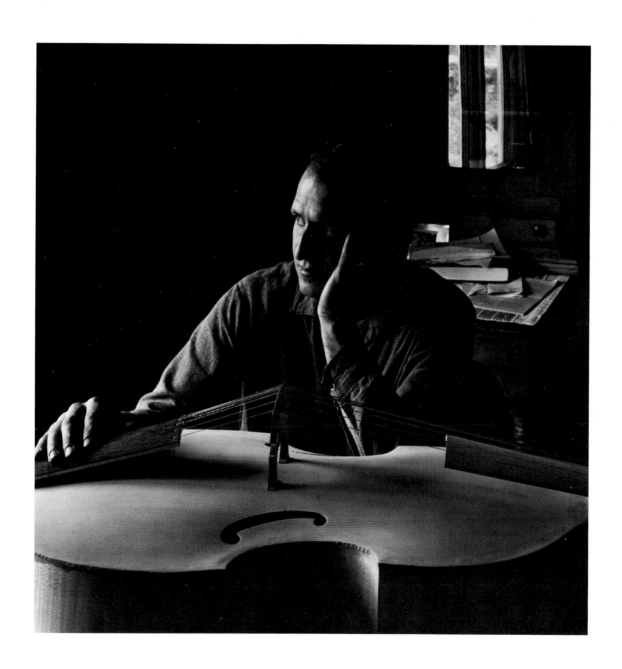

Dancer

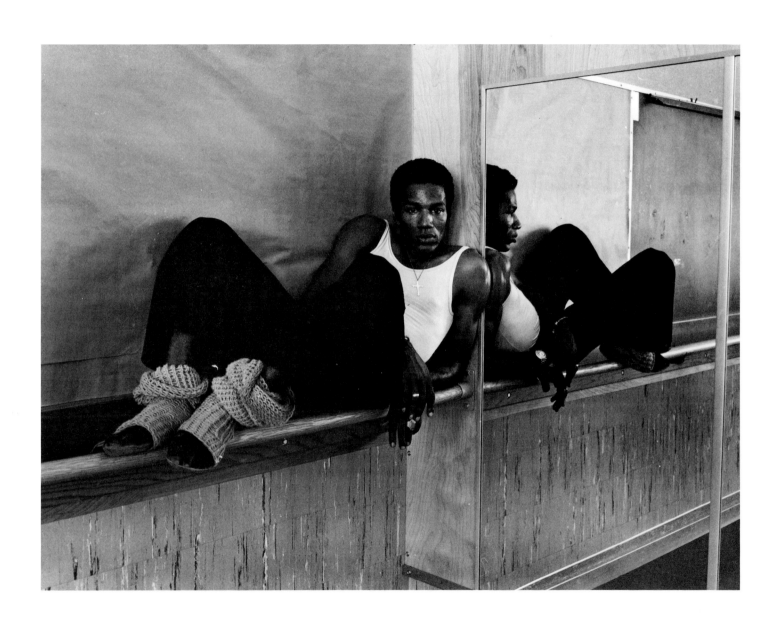

Photographer

When photographers get together they engage in two activities: talking shop and photographing one another.

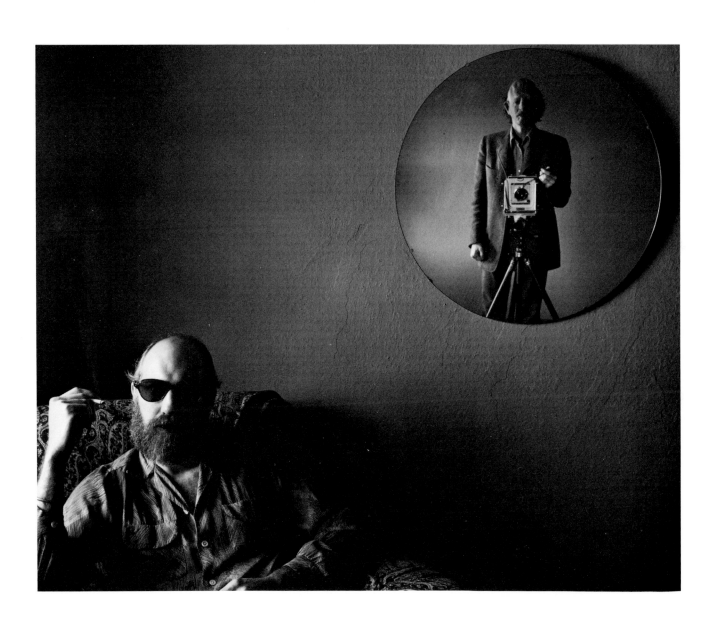

Donald

As the director of the Portland Art Museum he dresses appropriately: gray slacks, tweed coat and properly matched tie. A polite and formal person, he specializes in Oriental art. At home he's humorous and open. He lives in the country with his family in a cabinlike house with no electricity, heated by a wood stove and lit by kerosene lamps. His pride and joy is a huge garden which produces an incredible variety of vegetables and fruit.

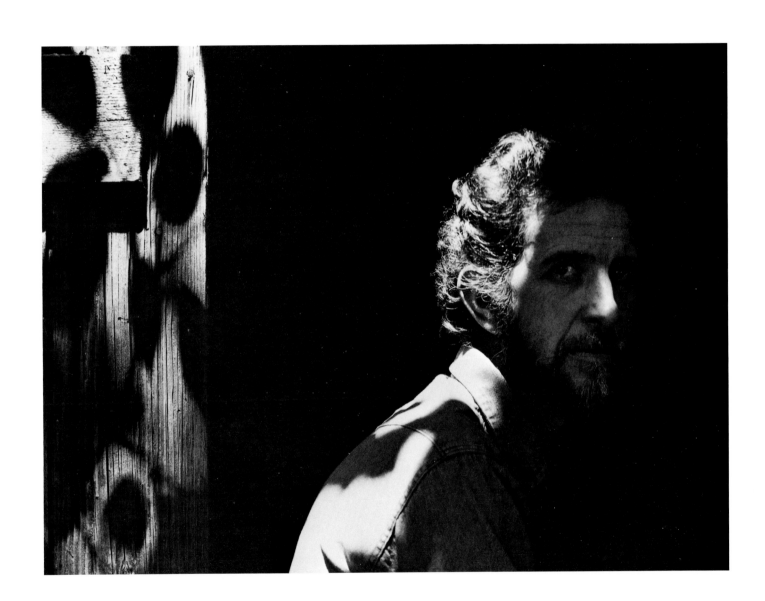

Unemployed Man

I had just finished a portrait of the hotel clerk. It was a dilapidated place with dark wood paneling, overstuffed chairs, old men and women—alone—staring at street traffic or watching the TV with its faded color and bad reception. This man asked me to take his picture so he could send copies to his mother in California. I agreed, but only if it was in his room. He looked nervous but he consented. So up we went. It was a tiny room, lit by a bare bulb above the sink. He went in first and I followed, closing the door behind me. Looking startled, he quietly worked his way around me back to the door and opened it enough for anyone passing to see what was going on—just picture taking, no hanky panky.

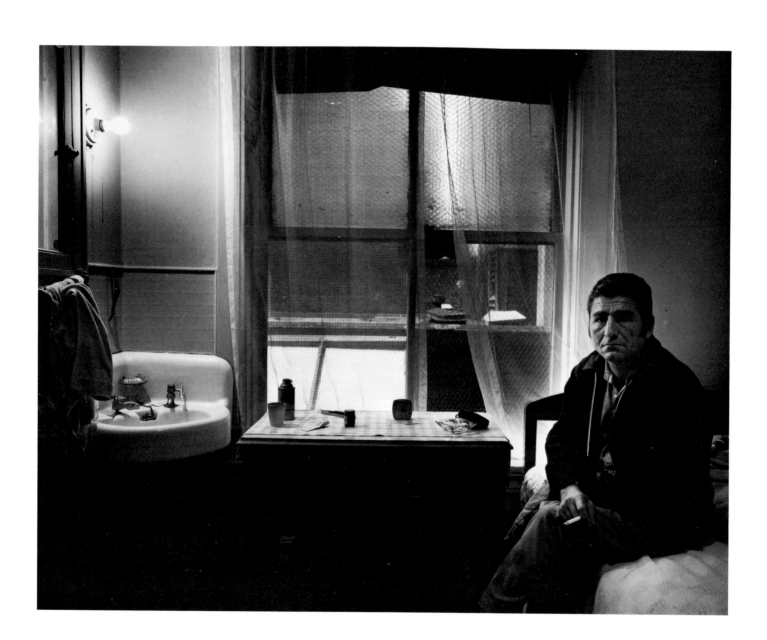

High School Students

For six months I taught at a high school that was predominantly black, and made portraits of the students. Interested in refining my vision, I made no more than one exposure of a sitter. I told this trio they had to pick the pose and let me know when they were ready.

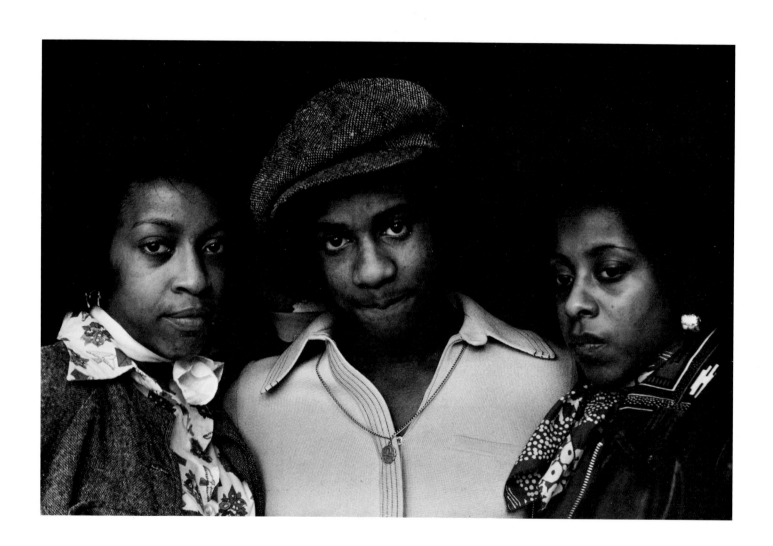

One-Ring Circus

This is the whole show: the performers and roustabouts. All that's missing are the three goats, two llamas, one pony, two bears (mother and cub) and ten pigeons. They perform under a pink-and-white canvas tent that has one ring and a seating capacity of sixty. They play the shopping-center parking-lot circuit around the Northwest. Some of these performers are just learning their trade, others are perfecting their acts, but all are biding their time, hoping to make it in a big-time circus. In a way, it's a circus school, run by the bald gentleman on the right. A strong and charismatic gypsy who spent many years in Kenya, he speaks four languages and trained the animals for the movies *Dr. Doolittle* and *Born Free*.

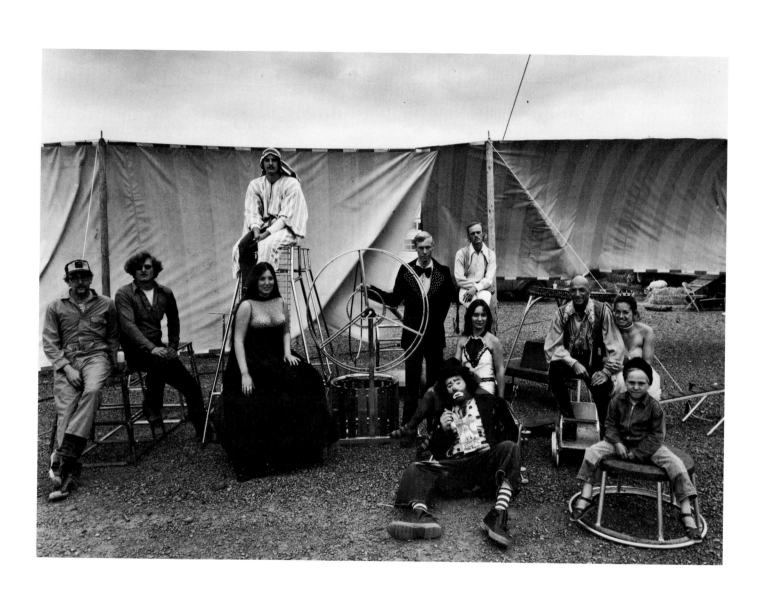

Retired Farmer

Driving through a small town, I passed this man sitting on a bench outside the only hotel, watching the traffic go by. He is as charming in person as he is on film.

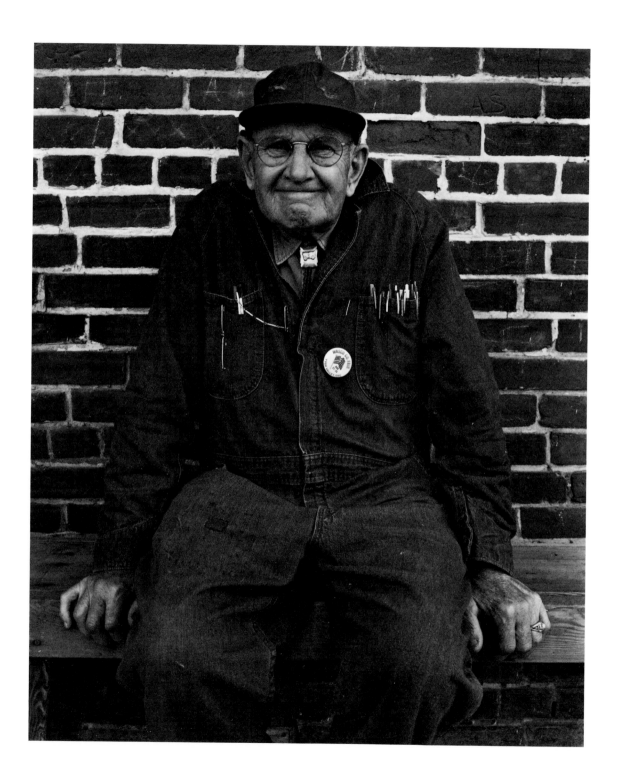

Friends

I first noticed them skating around the rink hand in hand, and when they came off I did this portrait.

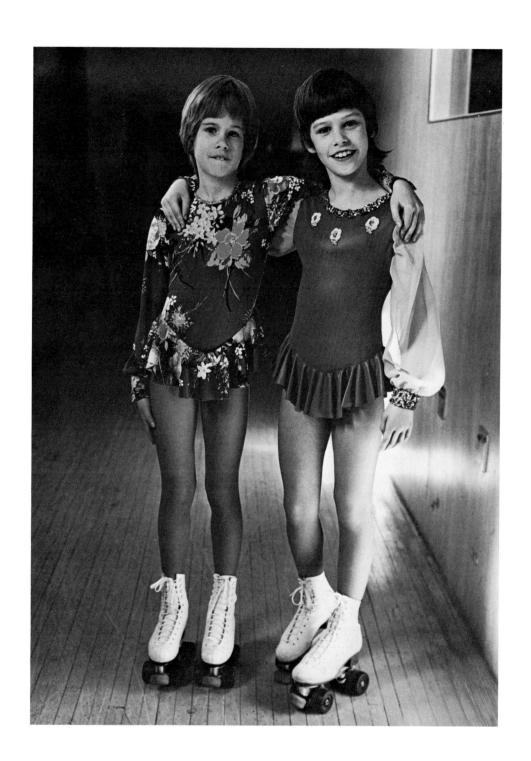

Frankie Saludo and Oscar

Frankie had been with Ringling Brothers' circus for years and was considered an institution among the performers. He thought he was the boss, and did he have a wicked temper! If anyone crossed him or made some comment that didn't sit well, Frankie would yell: "That's it for you, you're fired. I want you off the lot by tonight's show. If I see your face around here after that I'll call the cops." He'd storm off leaving the recipient of the tirade winking at the crowd that had gathered. The performers generally humored Frankie in these outbursts by either apologizing or staying out of his sight until he forgot the incident—usually within a day. His closest friend and companion was Oscar, the rabbit. He loved that animal.

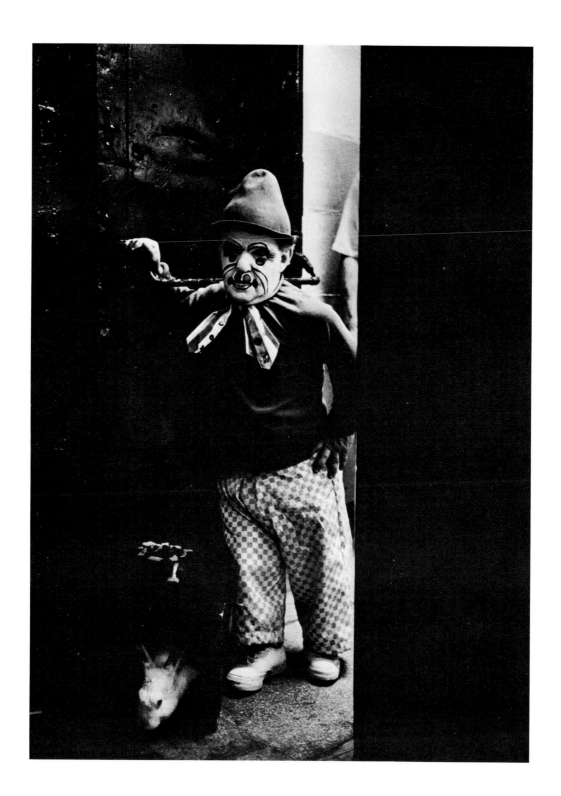

Mark

A long-time friend, he has gone through many changes since I first knew him. During the sixties and early seventies he was a committed political organizer and antiwar demonstrator. Since then he has been a facilitator in the human-potential movement, a counselor and a stockbroker. Now he's back in school working toward an M.S.W. in social services. His favorite animal and also his nickname is Rabbit.

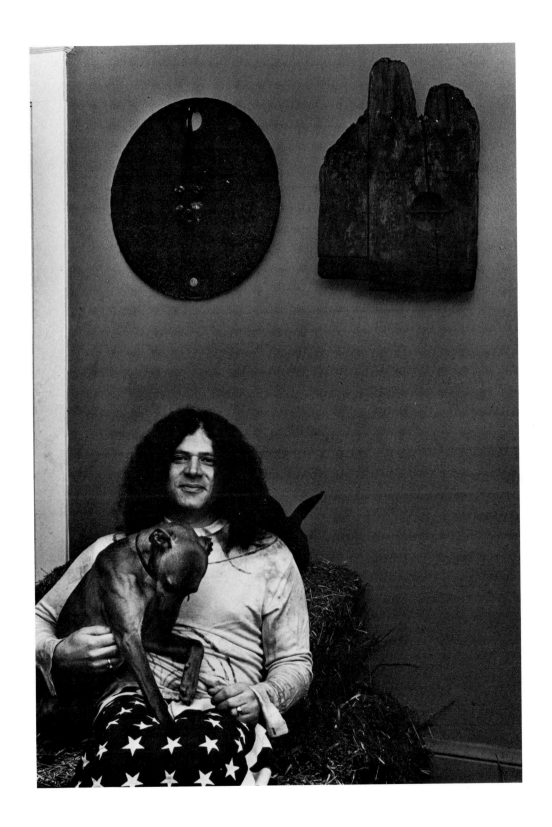

Bikers

Once a year a small town in Washington has a weekend of motorcycle races and becomes the rallying point for bikers from California and the Northwest. For two days it looks like the movie *The Wild Ones.* Main Street is lined with customized bikes and the bars are filled by nine in the morning. At night the street is blocked off to car traffic, and drunken riders impress each other doing wheelies up and down the main drag. I don't know why the town allows it—except for the money—but surprisingly, there's only drunkenness and fights, and very little property damage.

Saturday morning was gray and raining. The racetrack was all mud. Around it were campers, tents, and bikers drinking beer and having a good time. Away from the main activity I spotted two couples. I was hesitant, even scared, to approach them. I had seen motorcycle movies and read newspaper articles on such toughs. They would say no to pictures and maybe even break my face, or at least my gear. I figured the best approach was the most direct one, so I walked right up to them and delivered my spiel. To my surprise they were flattered. I wanted to do a portrait of just the men but as I was setting up, one of the women came over and said, "You ain't gonna take no picture of my old man without his old lady in it. It just don't look right." The guys looked a bit sheepish but didn't object.

Later that morning the sun came out and I went into town. I passed one bar with twenty choppers lined up in front. Just inside was a group of mean-looking bikers in their colors, drinking beer and carrying on in the soft morning light. As I stepped in to ask about a portrait an argument broke out. I asked for a beer instead. When things were quiet, I approached the bikers. Part of my rap is to offer free copies of everything I take. When I came to that part, the leader, Dirty Dan, interrupted, "You gonna give us prints or just proofs?"

"I usually just send proofs, but of course if I get a good picture that might warrant an eight-by-ten."

"Shit man, we *are* good pictures. You give us eight-by-tens of everything you take."

"No, that doesn't sound like a good deal to me. How about I'll make five prints plus the proofs. That's my best offer."

"It's a deal, man. How do you want us? We oughta be facing the door, the light's best there." When he gave the orders to the gang they started moving chairs, pushing tables and customers around to one side. This was to be a picture of the Bandidos only.

After a few shots Dan suggested I do some pictures of all of them by their machines. Out we went. He brought a barmaid with him and fondled her breasts. She wasn't sure what to do. I noticed a tourist across the street dressed in a blue double-knit suit who was taking pictures of the whole procedure with a telephoto. Cloverleaf, another gang member, saw the guy and began shouting, "You son of a bitch, what the fuck you think you're doing? Get out of my face or I'll come over there and shove that camera up your ass." The guy took off down the street.

When I finished we went back in the bar. Everyone was getting drunk and talking about the fun they would have fighting that night. I left.

I kept my word and sent them the proofs of what I had shot. A few weeks later I received a sweet and carefully handwritten letter from Dirty Dan, addressing me as Dear Sir. He formally thanked me for taking the time to do the portraits and wondered if it would be too much trouble to send along five eight-by-ten pictures he had chosen. For some reason he also returned the proofs. The letter was signed, "Yours truly, Dirty Dan."

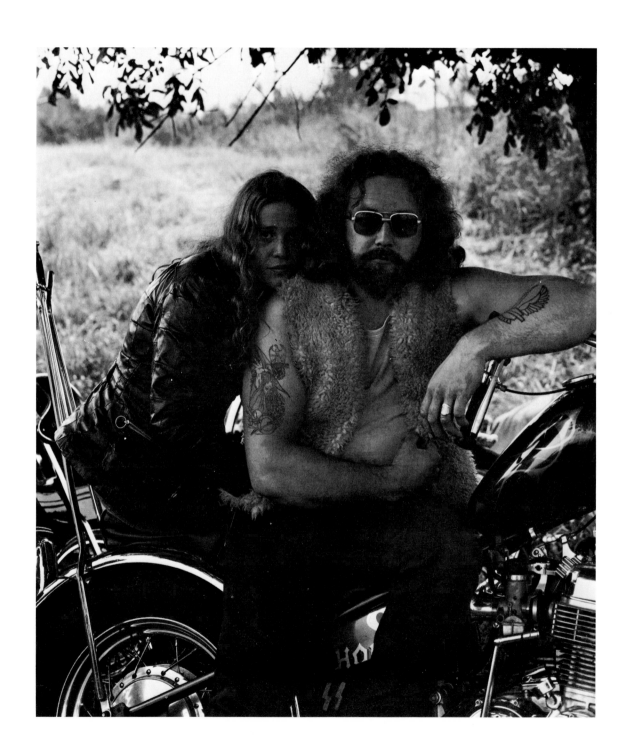

Carnival Fat Lady

The day was not a good one for her. The crowds had not been showing up as they should. The usual one-dollar admission—the cost of staring and gawking for ten minutes—had been cut in half. She was housed in a portable trailer, a large one with a porch on two sides and a small stairway leading up from the admission booth. Plate-glass windows covered one whole side and the back, and two brightly colored awnings doubled as shutters whenever the trailer was hauled to another carnival site.

My wife Andrea and I were the first ones up for the afternoon show. I took a position on the back window and began to set up the camera. Other people started to line up. The room was empty of Tiny Tina. There was only a large double bed covered with family photo albums and road maps. A handwritten sign tacked above the headboard read: "Do Not Ask Me To Stand." She emerged from a back room, looked at the people somewhat angrily and waddled to the end of the bed. She studied me for a while as I struggled with the four-by-five. "Are you a professional?" "Yes," I conceded. "Well, bring that contraption in here. You can't get a decent picture from behind that window. I need a good picture of myself to make a postcard to sell to customers. And bring your better half with you."

We went around to the back door and were let in. While Andrea and Tiny Tina carried on a conversation I made a handful of two-second exposures. She talked about her life. It was a living. Sure it was a drag, having people stare at you, but it paid the bills and you traveled and they're the freaks anyway. She would smile benevolently at the people behind the glass, all the time muttering, "The stupid bastards."

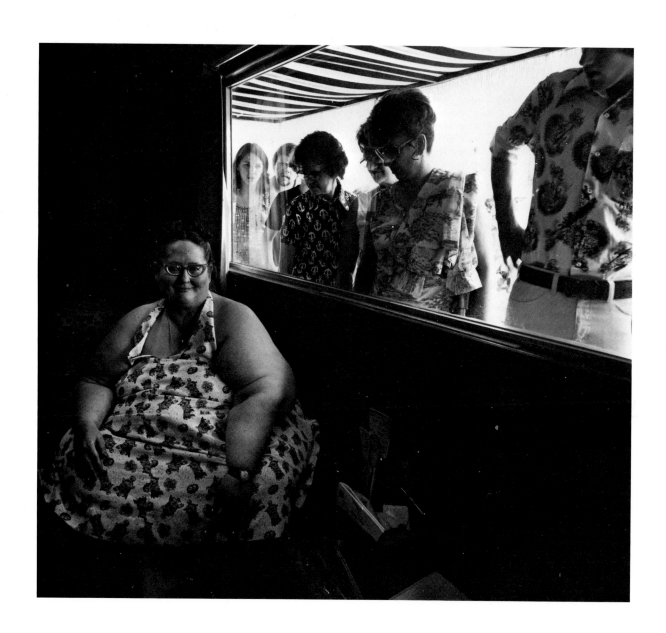

State Trooper

Wandering through some buildings at the Iowa State Fair, I stumbled upon the Iowa State Police exhibition. One wall of the room was covered with color photographs of car accidents, charred bodies of fire victims, and people who had been shot. Against the back wall was a life-size model of a local bedroom where a murder had occurred. Clothes were strewn around, a chair and bureau were overturned, and a lifelike female mannequin was sprawled across the bed. Her skull had been crushed, her throat cut and one knife wound had opened her stomach. The kitchen knife was sticking in her chest. Blood covered the seminaked body, sheets and bed.

On the third wall was this display case and the trooper, who passed out informational brochures and answered questions about becoming a policeman.

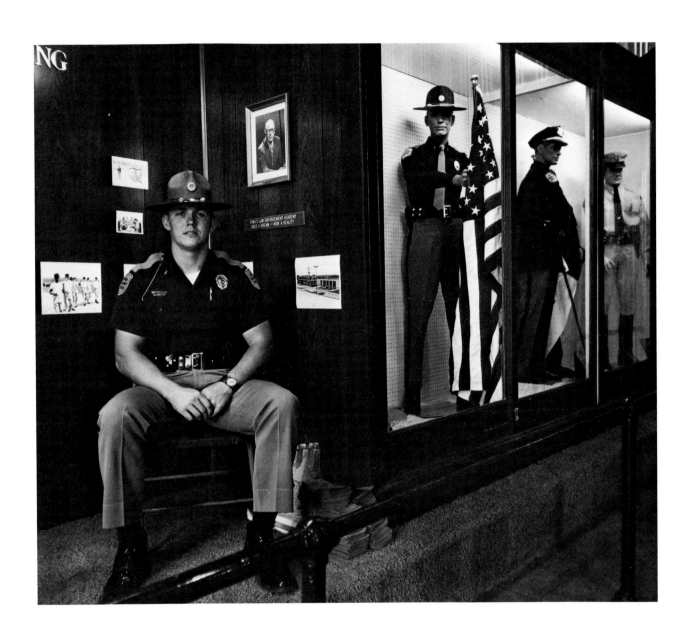

Film Maker

I've known Jim for years. He's balding, inventive, funny, eccentric and enjoys living in a mess. His refrigerator usually contains a few full bottles of beer plus several empty ones, a stick of margarine and some moldy cheese. When I went to do this picture, he had just purchased a four-gallon stewpot. He planned to make four gallons of soup each week and save on food. Another recent purchase he proudly showed me was a VW bus. The back had no seats; the floor was littered with film cans, dolly equipment, a shoulder brace, lights and a tripod. Generously sprinkled over all this were Big Mac wrappers and empty Kentucky Fried Chicken boxes.

He'd been working on a film called *Bird Woman*, and this was the mask for the leading lady.

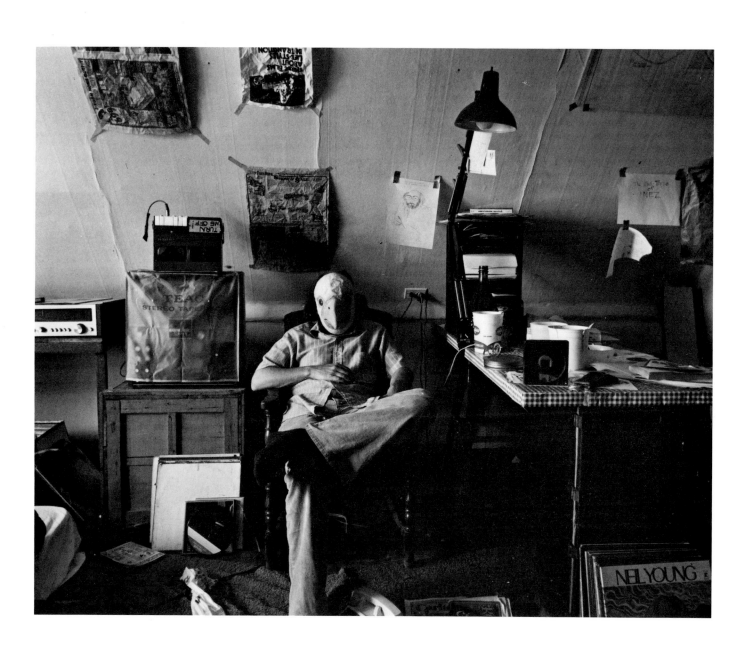

Dance Company

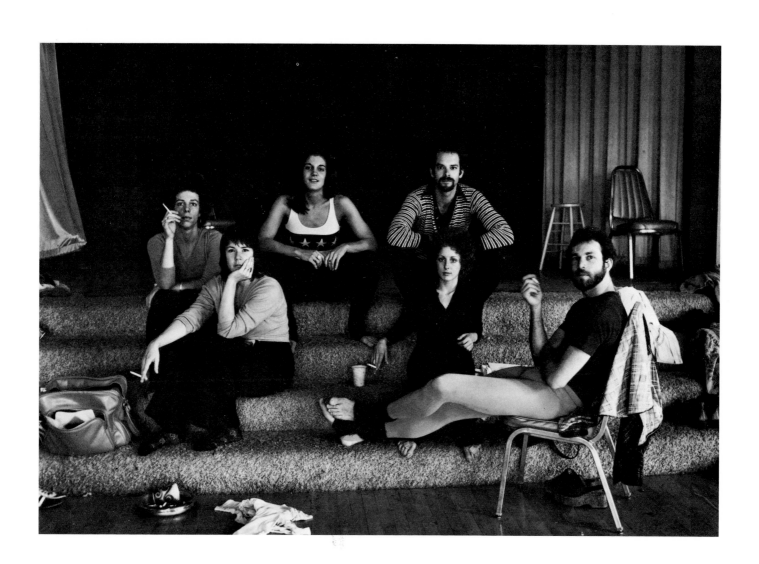

Retired Farmers: Fossil, Oregon

Driving through Fossil, a small, sleepy Oregon town, I saw these men. I turned the car around and passed the house again. There was no other traffic, and on my third conspicuous pass I decided to ask about a portrait. I had never been so aggressive in the country. As I was talking, their wives peeked out from behind the screen door. At first, the two men were reluctant. Gradually the one on the right began to enjoy the idea of having his picture taken, but was unable to persuade his friend. We talked about some ranches in the area. I had done a book on sheepherders from that part of the state. Once they knew I wasn't a total stranger to the country, they warmed up. I never did learn which man was Paul Rector.

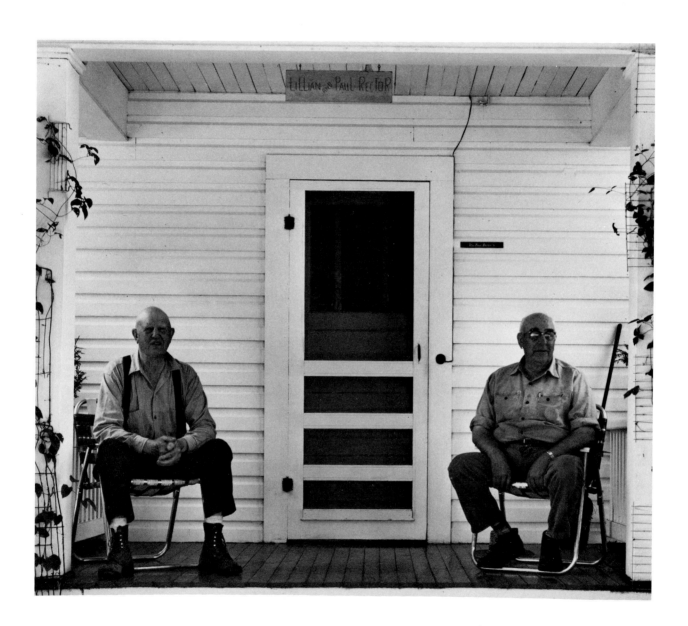

Teen-ager

The son of a doctor, he likes motorcycles, games, comics and smoking. I had just bought my first four-by-five and was running around making portraits of everyone I knew. I always wondered how he could sleep in that room.

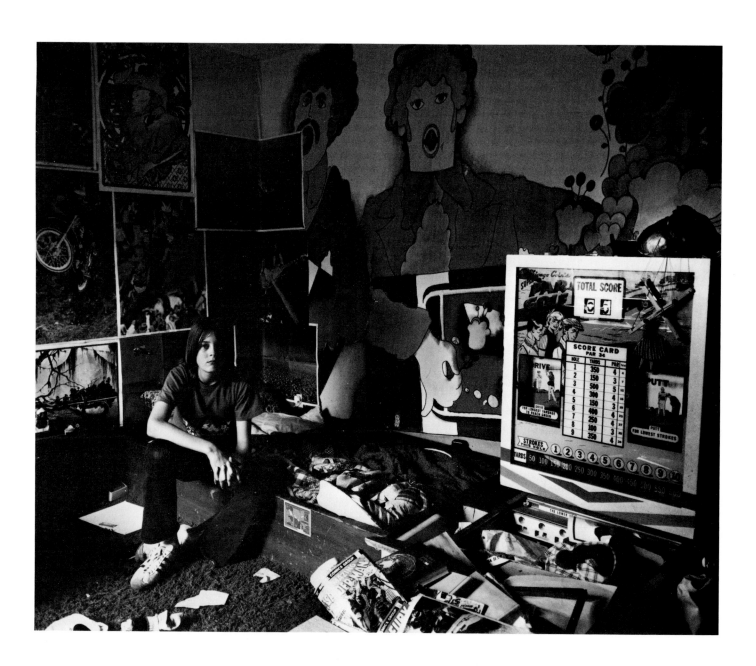

Family

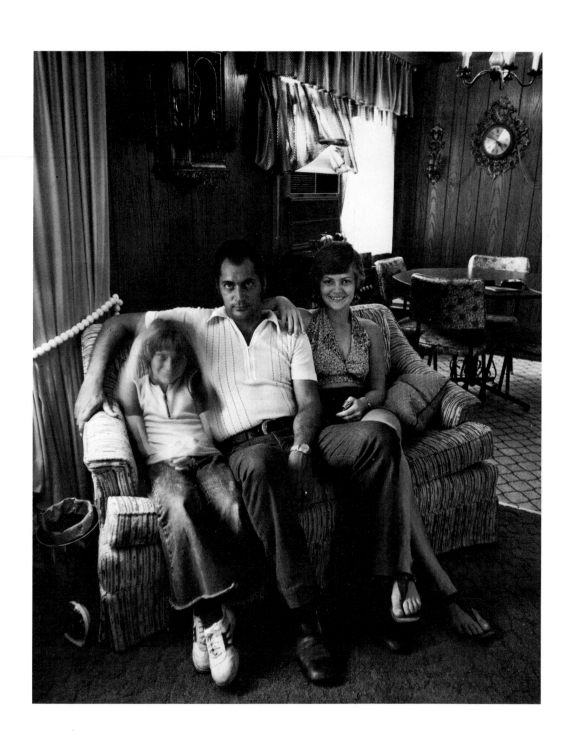

Porno Shop

The porno world is a clandestine one. The customers like to remain anonymous, slipping in and out of the gaudy doors either as secretly or nonchalantly as possible. This anonymity also holds true for the owners. The men behind the counters are just low-paid clerks, changing dollars to quarters for the arcades and selling movies, magazines and novelties to masturbate by. The owner is someone who comes in once a day at no specific time to clean out the cash register. I learned this after visiting all the shops in Portland and asking each clerk if I could do a portrait. Most said no. I had to have the permission of the owner, whose identity they were unwilling to divulge. It wasn't until I hit Sin City that this man gave me the name and address of the owner, who, as it turned out, owned three-quarters of all the places in the city or was managing them for someone who operated out of Los Angeles.

The address was in the industrial area. With some difficulty I located the number scrawled in chalk on the brown, dingy door of a building in which cardboard boxes were manufactured. I somehow expected a more impressive front for such a money-making operation. I rang the bell and was let into an anteroom with a cashier's booth encased in bars at one end. The woman there asked who I wanted to see. The owner. About what? Photography. She talked to someone on the intercom, nodded me to the door on the left and rang a buzzer that let me into a long hallway. "Go down to the last office on the right." There were no windows. I was closed off from the natural world in the bowels of this industrial building. The first two offices were closed but the last one was a small cubicle with a desk taking up most of the room. Behind it sat a hulk of a man, bulbous nose, carbuncular face, black wary eyes. He wore a short-sleeve Hawaiian shirt and a yellow cap that had *Caterpillar* written on the front. He looked like a hit man from an old Hollywood movie. Cellophane-wrapped dildos, fuck movies and deflated blow-up dolls covered the floor. I had entered the heart of the city's porno business and I was scared. He told me to come in. I had to step over a pile of eight-inch rubber penises to stand in front of him. I started to explain my presence, but as soon as I mentioned I was a photographer, he interrupted. "You do color? Slides? Movies? You got something for me to see or you looking for work?" Oh my, was I in the wrong place. Well, what the hell, all he could do was throw me out, I hoped. So real briefly I described what I wanted. He just looked at me, eyes narrowed. A long pause, then, "Fuck, no."

I left but I had spent too much time not to get a portrait, so back to Sin City. I told the clerk what had happened. He was sympathetic. Since he planned to quit in a week, he wouldn't mind being photographed, but it was nearly time for the boss to pick up the day's earnings. Hurriedly I set up and made a few exposures. Each time the door opened I was sure it would be the Caterpillar man and that would be it for me. That portrait was one of the quickest I've ever done—about six minutes. I later learned that this gentleman was a member of the Great Book Society and a chamber music aficionado.

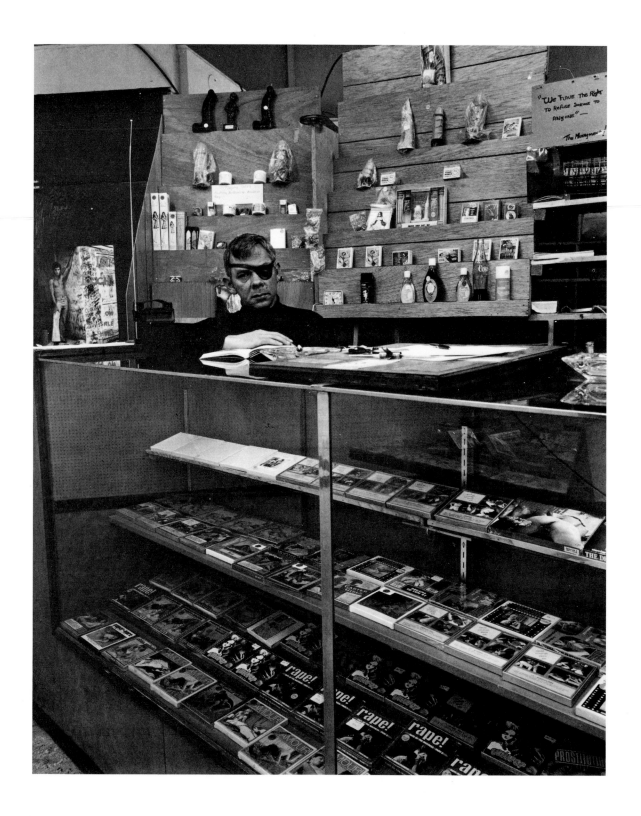

Bruce

Bruce is a commercial photographer, a patient friend and an insightful critic of my work. I run in and out of his life and studio asking technical questions, showing new prints and occasionally doing portraits of him. During one of my hectic visits I wanted to experiment with a new approach to portraiture, at least to me—the use of dark areas to add mystery and drama. I went in the back room and saw this pattern. The sun was setting and I had only about four minutes before the light faded. I grabbed him out of the darkroom and he patiently posed.

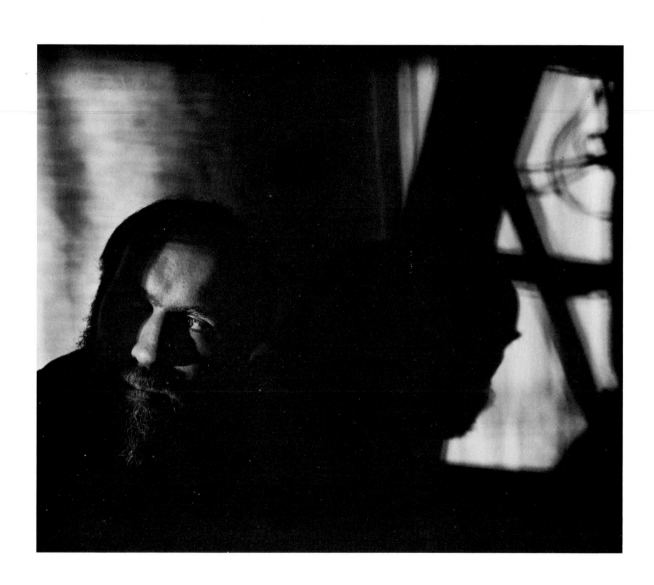

John and Nicole

My brother's first child.

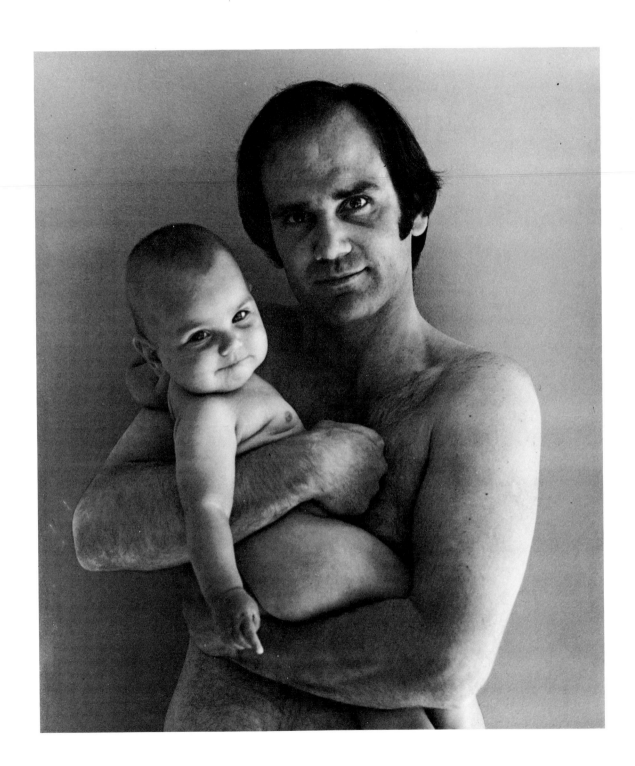

Lilla

A child prodigy in Europe, she gave her first concert at the age of twelve. A gifted musician with both the viola and violin, she studied with the masters. She felt she could have done better, even been great, but she didn't practice enough. She had been given this gift or, as she put it, music had chosen her, but she didn't have the dedication for daily practice. She had misused her talent. Even now, at seventy-three and only recently retired, she still castigated herself for not practicing. To her, she had wasted her talent, but her life had been filled with intense personal relationships and politics.

She was a good friend of Gretel, my collaborator and companion, and Gretel and I interviewed her for a book. We spent two wonderful evenings talking about our creative work: both the dry spells and the times it becomes all-consuming. Usually when someone is interviewed, the conversation turns into a monologue, but not with Lilla. The interview became a dialogue among the three of us. Rarely do I meet someone for the first time with whom I immediately feel close and at ease. She is one of those people. Though I have spent only two days with her, she will always have a place in my heart.

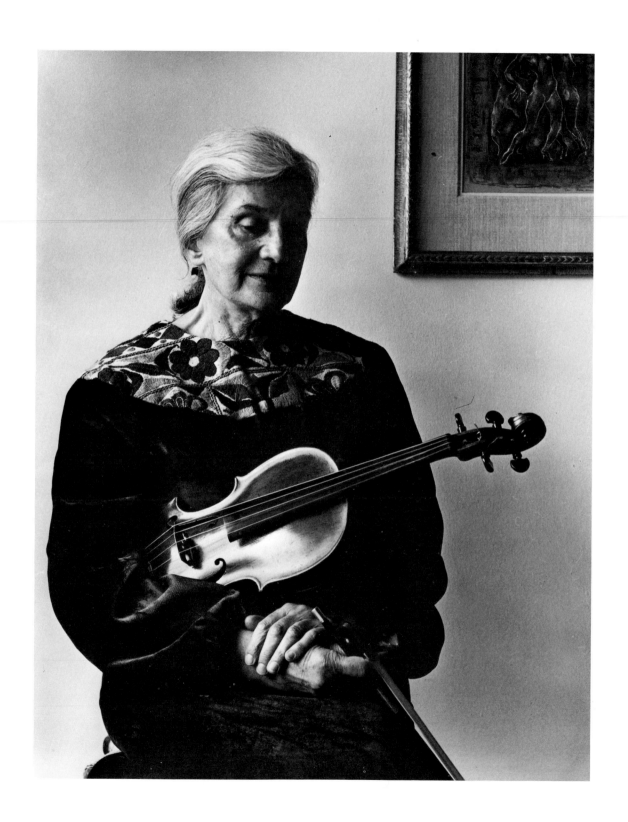

Ellen

She lives on a ranch in Montana, forty miles from the nearest town. Born in the East, she first came west as a child on a family vacation and fell in love with the land. She knew she belonged there—had to live there. It took many years, plus the family's disapproval, to get back. She eloped with a composer and drove a Model T coast to coast in just six days back in the thirties. They lived in northern California for several years until the marriage dissolved. She returned to her first love, Montana, and worked on ranches until she met Duane, a cowboy. They married and bought a ranch and worked it together until he died. For the past fifteen years she has been running it, primarily by herself, except during the summer when young people from all over the country flock there to help with the haying.

She runs about four hundred head of cattle, numerous horses, chickens, cats, dogs and three milk cows. Her day is made if she can ride for a couple of hours in the morning. An independent woman, strong and at times ornery, she has been fighting strip mining in the West, especially in Montana. She can't stand to see the land ruined.

I had heard about her all through college from her niece, a friend of mine. The year I graduated I traveled through South and Central America. On my way back east I decided to hitchhike through Montana and pay her a surprise visit. I got a ride up to the ranch road and walked the last mile. As I neared the house the dogs began to bark: one collie, a mutt and three dachshunds. The porch door opened and out she came. Without a word or hesitation she ran up and gave me a big bear hug, knapsack and all. "You must be Mike." A most enjoyable welcome, since we had never met before. I spent several days there, in which time she introduced me to Tchaikowsky and to Jimmy Rogers, the singing brakeman, a folksinger from the thirties who sang songs about hobos and the working man.

That was over ten years ago, and whenever I'm in her neck of the woods, I visit. The last time I visited I made this portrait. She talked a lot about strip mining and her love for the land. Late one evening after supper she told a story about one of her dogs, Spook, who had been a constant companion for over fifteen years. He was arthritic and nearly blind but, surprisingly enough, he could still get excited by a female in heat, excited but nonfunctioning. Finally his hind legs gave out and he had to be destroyed. She carried him out to the porch, where she had carefully concealed a rifle, and sat with him. Then she produced some liver, and when he was busy eating, his back to her, she shot him.

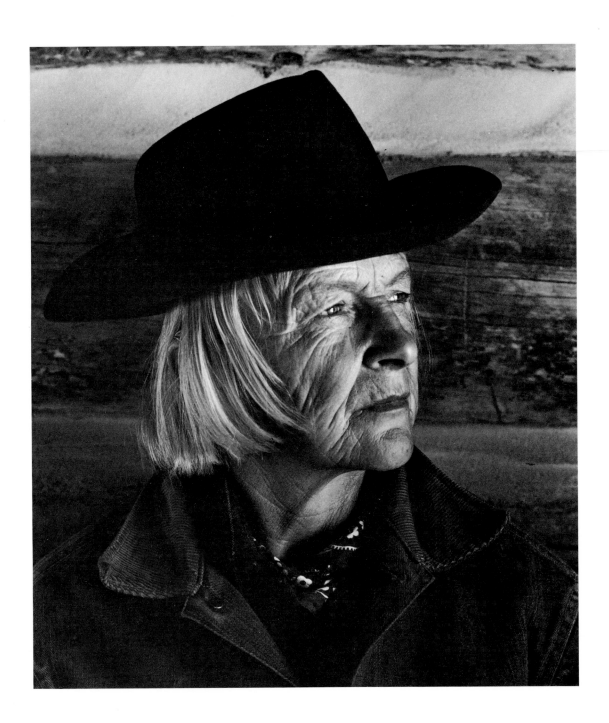

Cathy

A doll collector for several years, she had just reached
the stage where she was interested in boys.

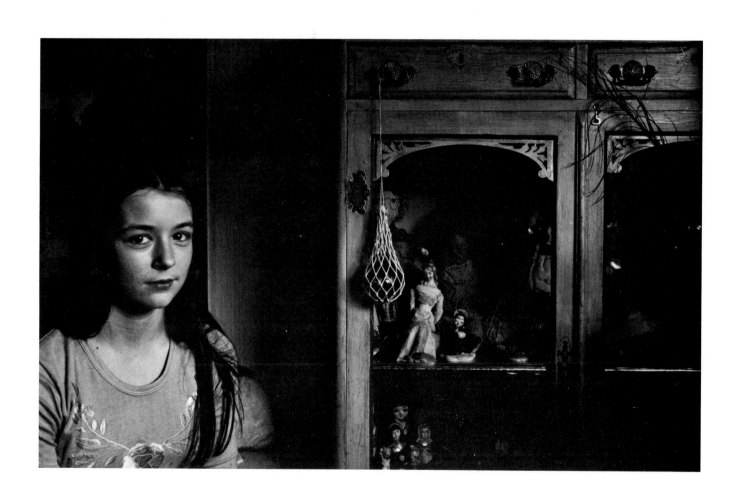

Kathy

She is an old friend of my former wife. She stayed with us for several months on a farm outside Portland, which gave the neighbors something to talk about. Before coming to Oregon, she had been politically active in Cleveland, organizing factory workers and working on a community newspaper, but she became discouraged with the lack of progress and the infighting that went with working on a paper. She lived with us while she planned her next move. This portrait was done during that hiatus in her life. I've always liked it because I felt it showed an inner peace and strength that she hadn't found before.

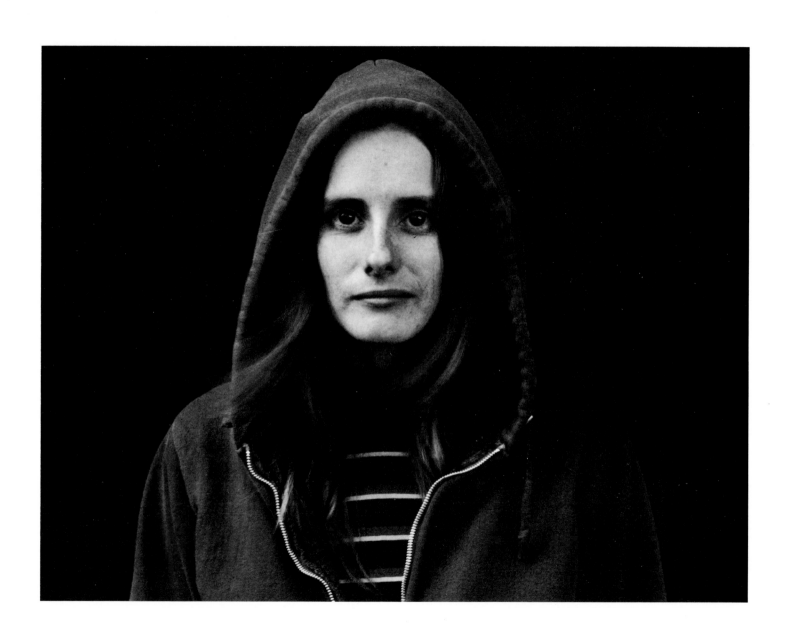

Marlene

She always reminded me of David Bowie.

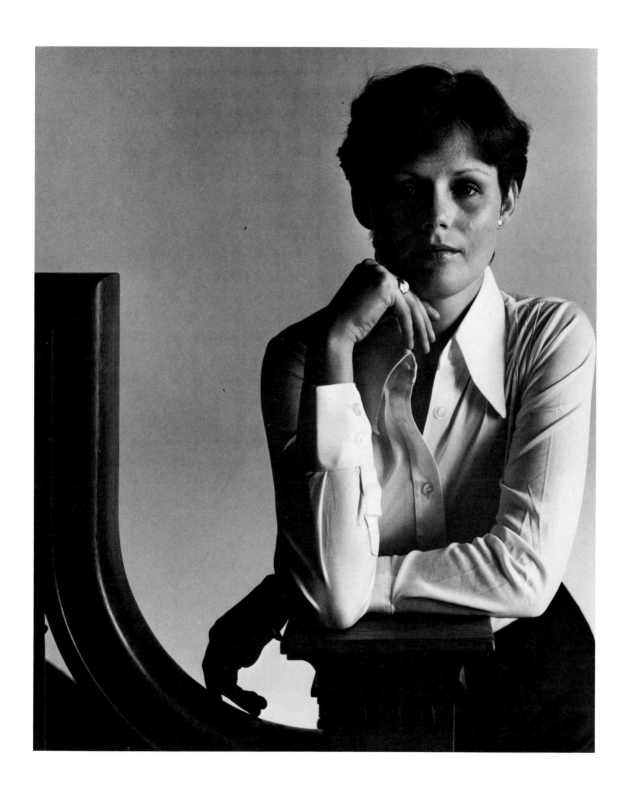

Billy

Billy is a dancer and friend. He wanted some pictures of himself dancing so he could study his form. In exchange he posed for some portraits I wanted to do.

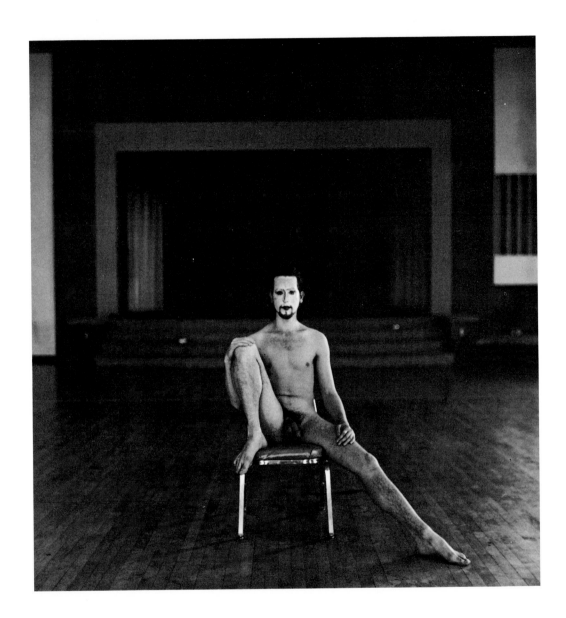

Drag Queen and Escort

Each fall in Portland, a faction of the gay community hosts the Empress Coronation Ball. At this gala event the reigning Empress of the Inland Empire presides over the final night of festivities for the year, before passing on the crown to her successor.

When I first heard about this party all I knew about drag queens was from photographs, which generally depicted them as freaks or, at the very least, lonely and isolated people. I knew there was more to them than that cliché. So I decided to do some portraits at the ball. I set up lights and the camera in a back room away from the main activity. I wanted to work in a one-on-one situation so the subjects would be reacting to me, not to other queens. During the evening I went to the ballroom and asked various men if they'd be interested in a portrait. Of the entire group of pictures, this is my favorite. It shows the humor and the enjoyment of that night.

After several hours of doing portraits, I decided to wander around with a small candid camera. The scene was bizarre enough, with everyone participating in his own fantasy, so that I felt I could do something I'd always wanted to do in public—talk to myself. I went about carrying on a monologue about exposures, composition and the indoor weather. No one noticed or, more to the point, no one cared. It was a wonderful night.

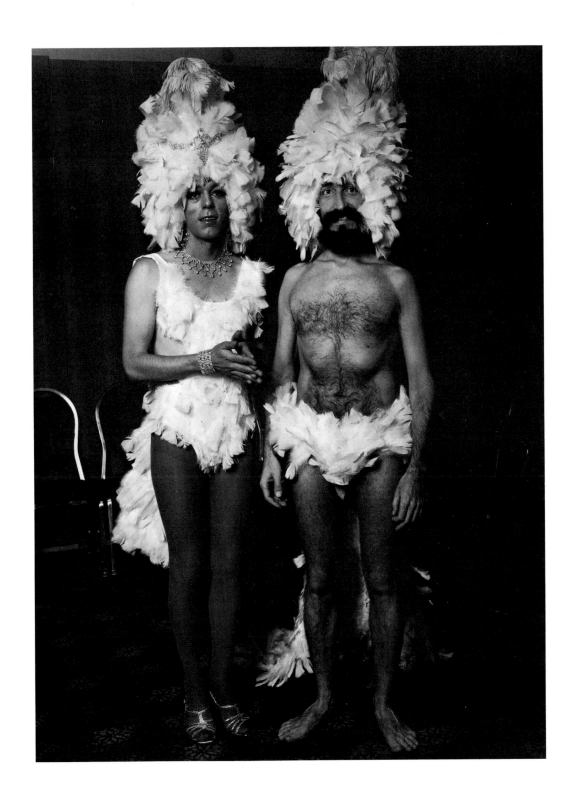

Wrestler

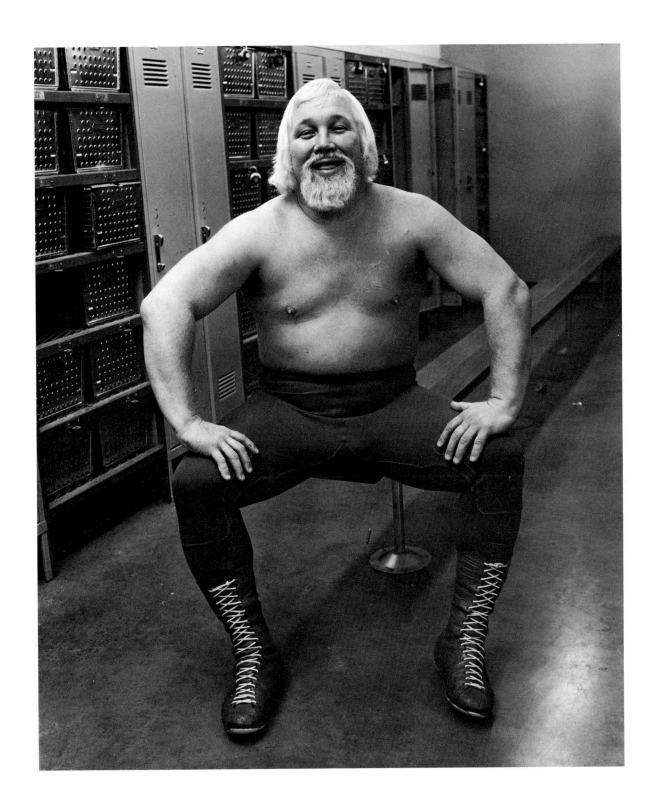

Tillie

Every Sunday evening at seven in a small, unobtrusive two-story green house on a dead-end street, about twenty people gather in Tillie's living room to hear her give aura readings. The three overstuffed chairs that usually take up a good portion of the living room have been put against the wall to make space for twenty wooden folding chairs that are placed in three rows. A stand-up piano is in one corner, the top covered with pictures of Tillie's children and grandchildren, a framed color photograph of her and her husband smiling on their fiftieth wedding anniversary. A large black-and-white picture of Christ rests on the ledge above the keyboard. Her portable pulpit has been pulled out from behind the front door to face her congregation.

She has been holding these Sunday meetings for thirty-five years. Until five years ago, when he died, she worked with her husband. Most of the people there are older women, friends who have been coming for years. Occasionally they bring young relatives—a niece, nephew or grandchild. And each week there are a few new faces, usually in their twenties—couples or hippies who have heard about her and are curious. I was one of the curious.

People mill around and make small talk until Tillie stands beside the pulpit. Then, silence. She begins by reading from the Bible. A gentle person, she has a voice that is soft and subdued. After the Bible reading she gives the aura readings. Looking at someone for a moment, she closes her eyes and starts talking. It's a different voice—lilting and strong. Words pour out as if there's no conscious thought, no premeditation, as if she's a channel. One by one, she describes the colors of the aura surrounding everyone there and talks about their present situation, focusing on the strong points of their lives or personalities. Very little time is spent on anything negative. She goes around the room doing this for each person.

After the meeting as people were leaving, I asked if I could do a portrait of her sometime. She was quite hesitant and said that she didn't want publicity—she wasn't special, just doing the Lord's work. She also mentioned that she saw a black spot over my heart. That got to me. I knew what she was talking about. I had come there because I had heard that this old woman gave these readings and it sounded a bit bizarre and I had hoped I could get it on film. I felt totally transparent in front of this frail woman, caught in my own dishonesty.

After that I visited her several times alone, just to talk, and discovered a shy, humble and reverent woman who was doing her appointed work. On my last visit she allowed me to make this portrait.

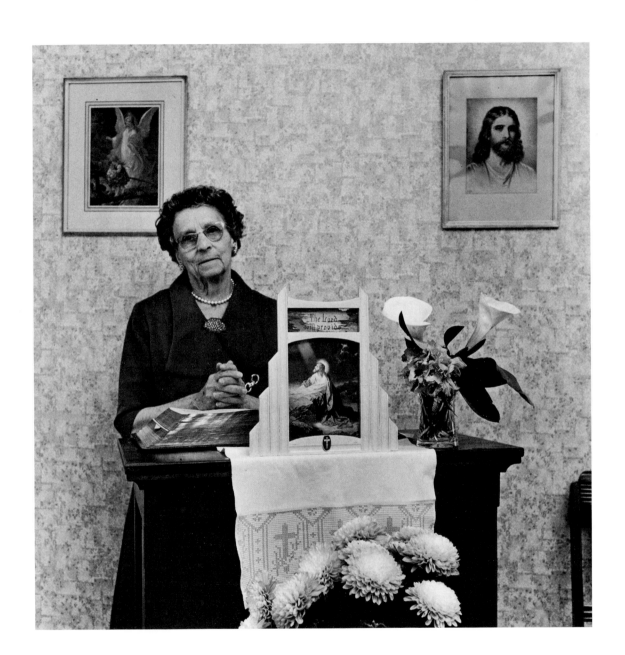

Marion

A kind and generous woman who had recently begun making photographs. We see each other to exchange photographic notes, talk and make portraits.

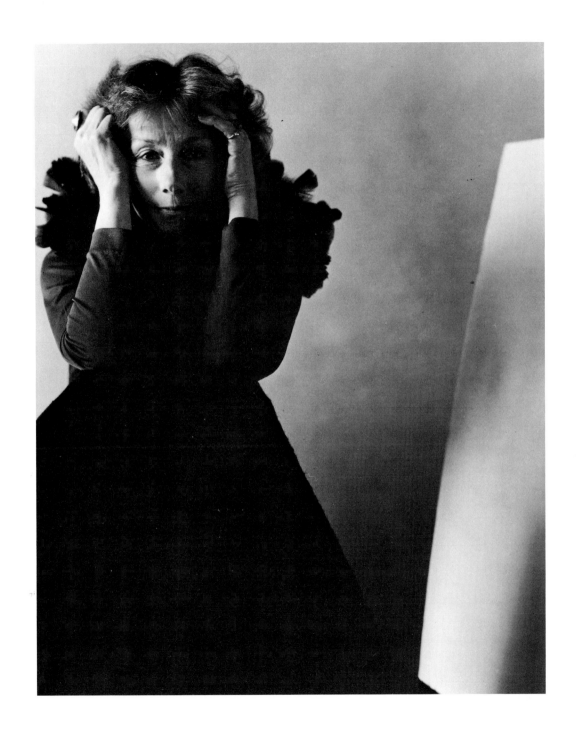

Orlando

He's a hairdresser by trade and occasionally likes to get dressed up in drag. Unlike many other queens he doesn't wear flashy sequined gowns, ornate wigs or heavy make-up. His clothes are elegant and tasteful and he's one hell of a looker when he's all "cranked up."

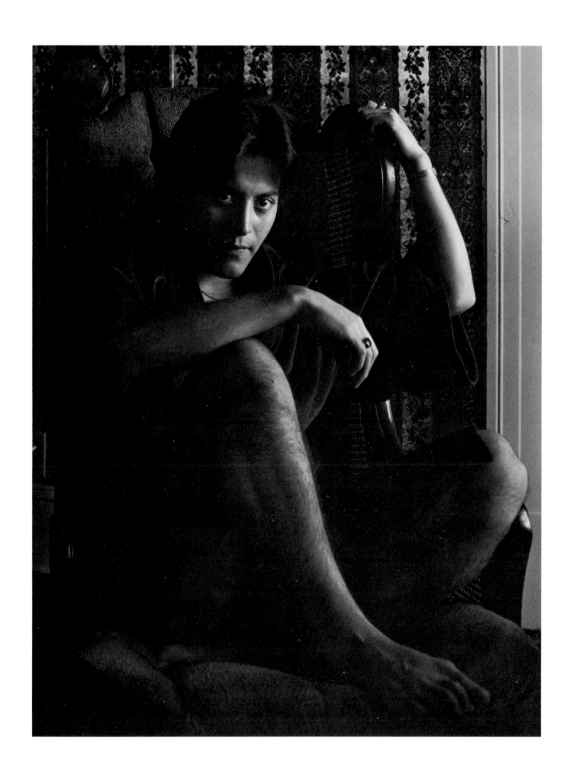

Addison

Describing Addison is a difficult task. To do it very briefly I'd call him a modern day prophet. He lives with his wife and three Chihuahuas in a ranch-style house on the outskirts of a black neighborhood. The paint is peeling on three sides; the fourth side has been scraped and is ready for the primer but it's been that way for years. All the windows are covered with bed sheets or old drapes. In the driveway sits an old VW bus, four flat tires, filled with manuscripts. The ground floor is totally covered with antiques, piles of junk and books; two narrow paths have been cleared between the debris, one from the front door around a large bookshelf to a sofa on which his wife sleeps and watches TV, and the other from the sofa back to the kitchen. Even the bathroom is a storage space, the bathtub overflowing with magazines and pamphlets, the shower curtain rod serving as a clothesline for an assortment of dresses and suits.

Addison makes his living as a machinist in a large industrial plant. He has the graveyard shift and rides to work on a small Honda motorcycle year-round. In his spare time he reads philosophical treatises and writes about ways to solve the world's problems. He's incredibly well read and a most articulate man, but I never could really understand his writing.

He prints his manuscripts on a press in the cellar and staples them into books. The basement is stacked ceiling high with his unread work. He sleeps on an army cot beside the press. He is considered something of a nut by local people in his field, but that doesn't faze him—he thinks all prophets have been ahead of their time: "John the Baptist was undoubtedly an unwashed long-haired hippie freak."

I spent an afternoon doing portraits. A space had to be cleared so that I could set up my tripod. The chair used to belong to Theodore Roosevelt. The entire time, he talked about what had gone wrong in the world and various solutions to the problems, but I was unable to keep up with him. The three miniature dogs barked and lapped coffee from my cup when I wasn't looking.

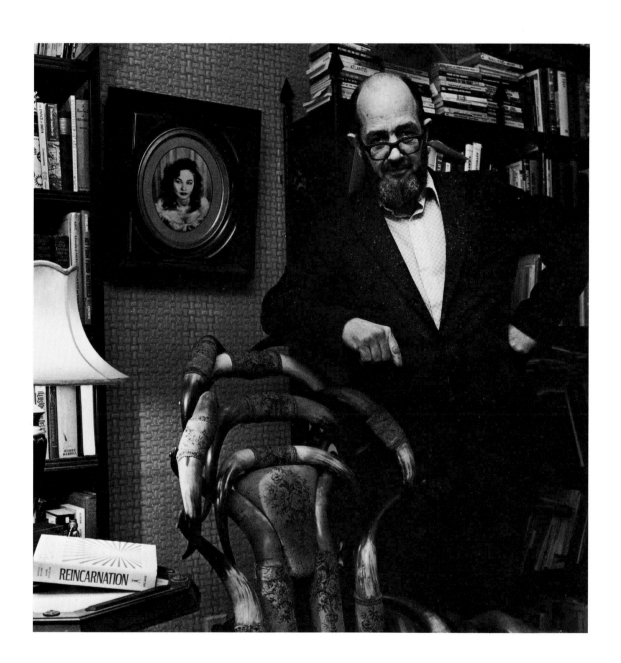

Steve

He's a professional housesitter for the wealthy in the San Francisco area. The son of an itinerant farmer from Texas, he has always sought out the cultured life. He found his way to California and hobnobs with local artists and writers. He lives in the lap of luxury, but is virtually broke. Impeccably dressed, he gets his clothes from carefully picked-over racks at Salvation Army and second-hand stores. Never without a monogrammed shirt—no two have the same initials—he can fit all his belongings into a seaman's duffle bag.

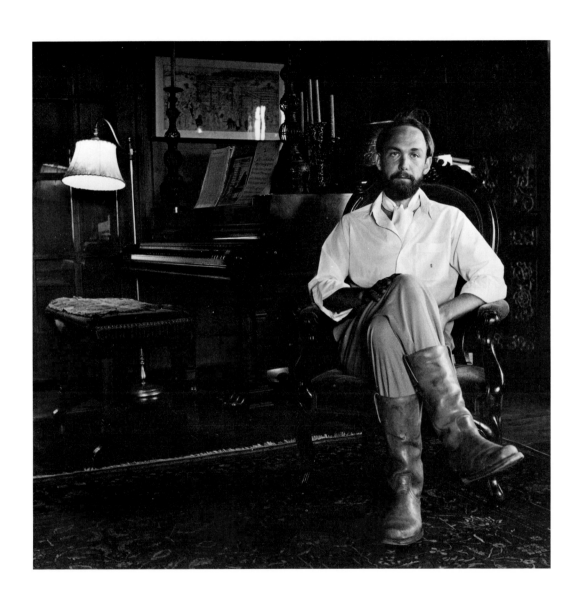

Lion Tamer

Ever since Roger can remember he wanted to be a lion tamer. As a teen-ager he managed to land a job with Clyde Beatty, the man who made the cat act famous in the circus. Roger was his shit shoveler and general gofer. Over the years he learned the trade and eventually started his own act. His outfit is an exact replica of the one Beatty always wore.

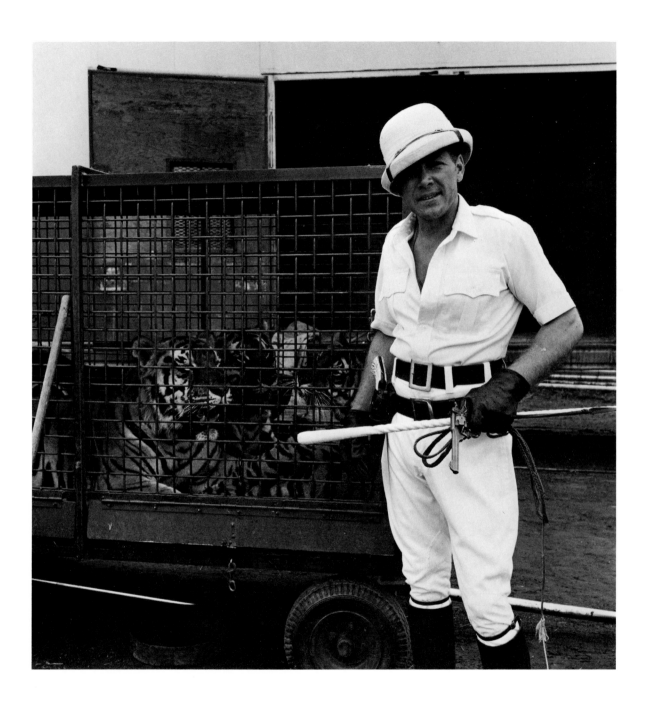

Retired Couple

They live in Kildeer, North Dakota and have spent most of their lives there, he as a postal clerk and she as a mother and secretary. Occasionally they venture to South Dakota, Iowa or Minnesota to visit relatives.

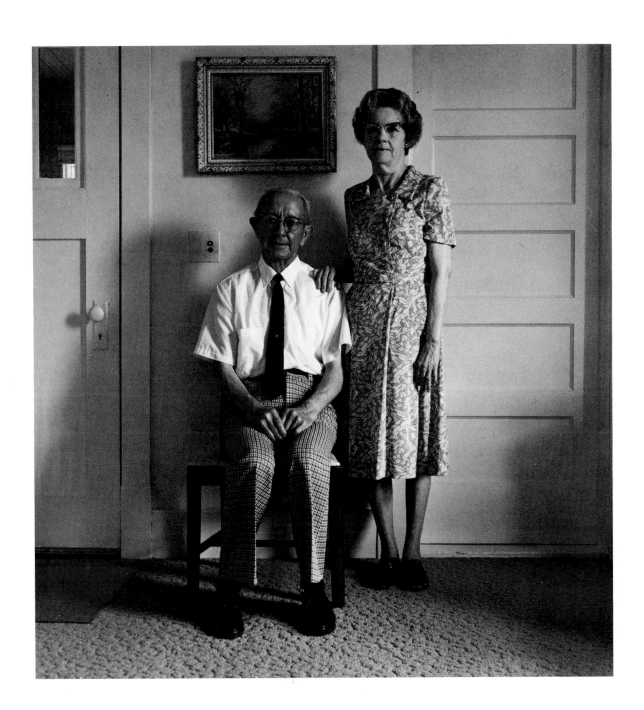

Slaughterhouse

I made the mistake of wearing sandals that day. After I did some individual portraits, the foreman asked if I would do a group shot. I reluctantly agreed, figuring I couldn't use such a picture because it would look like a publicity shot. As I set up he dropped a steer from the hook onto the cutting bars and cut off the head and forefeet. They lined up behind the carcass.

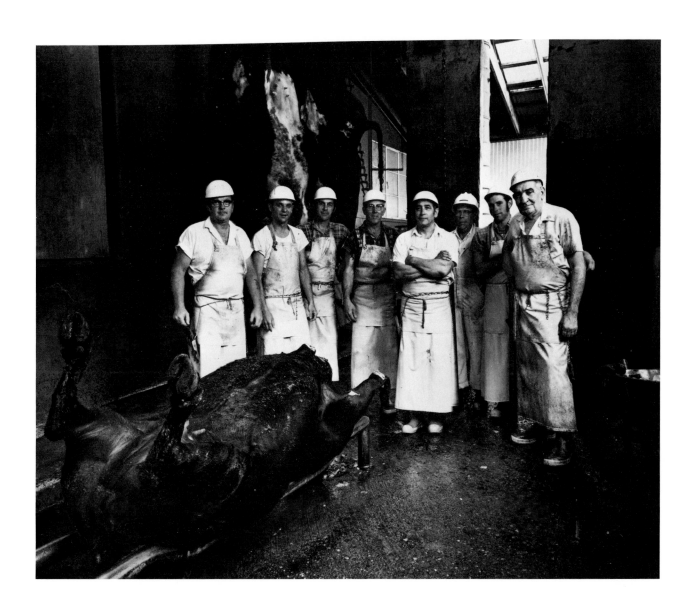

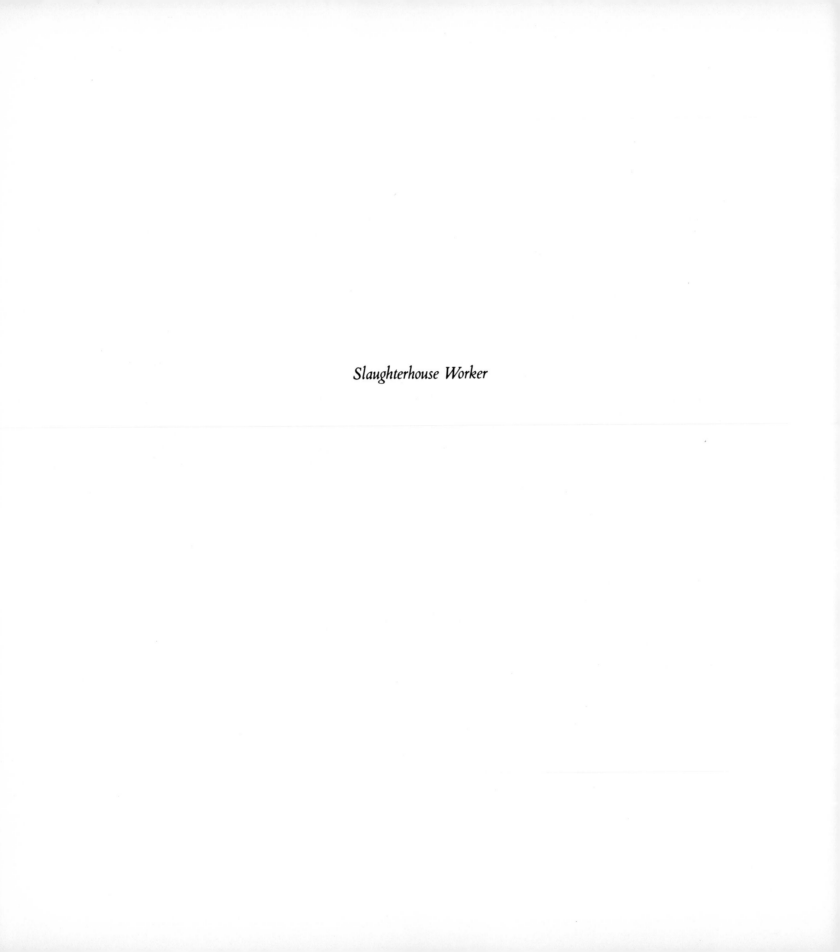

Slaughterhouse Worker

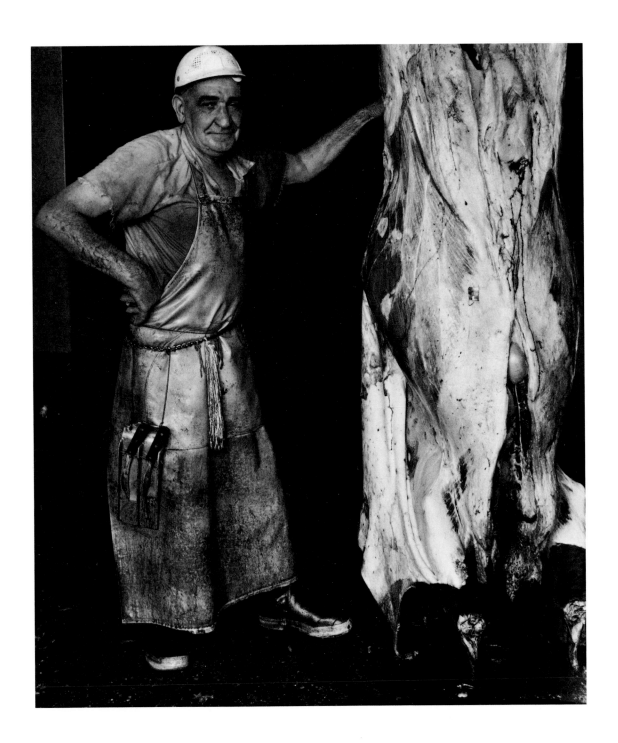

Sawmill Operator

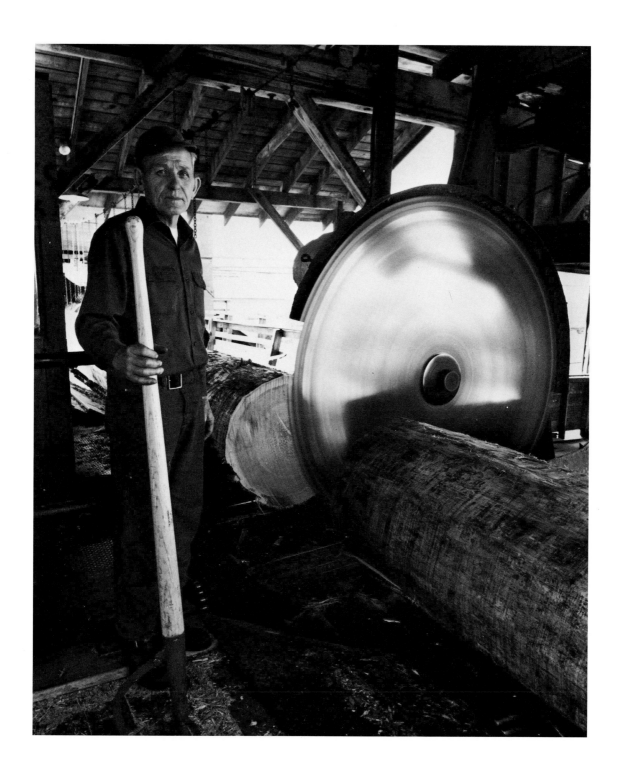

Big Ed, Copper Miner

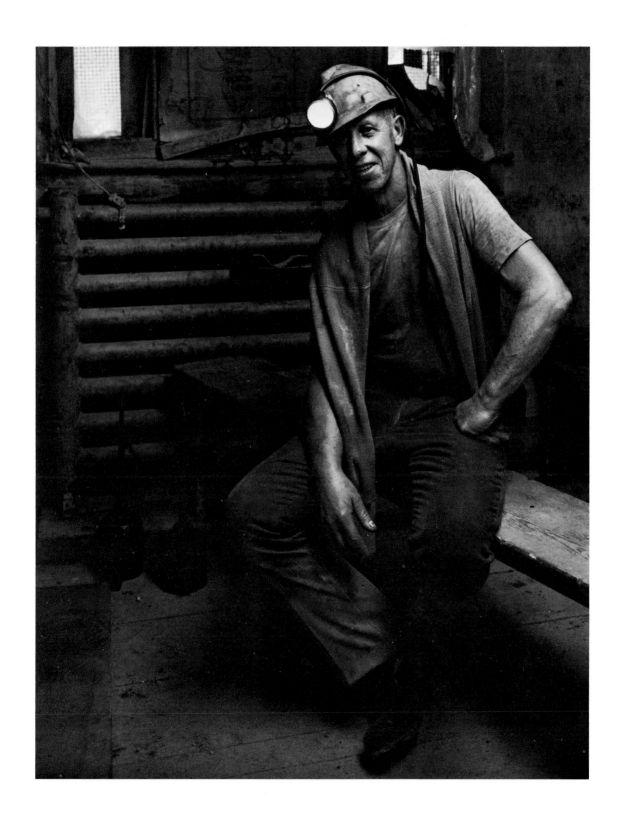

Lime Factory

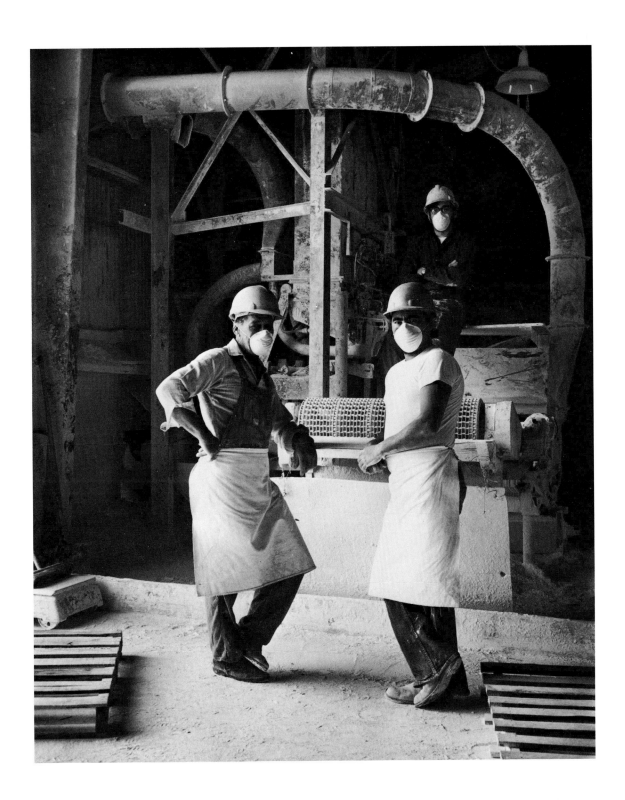

Motorcycle Mechanic

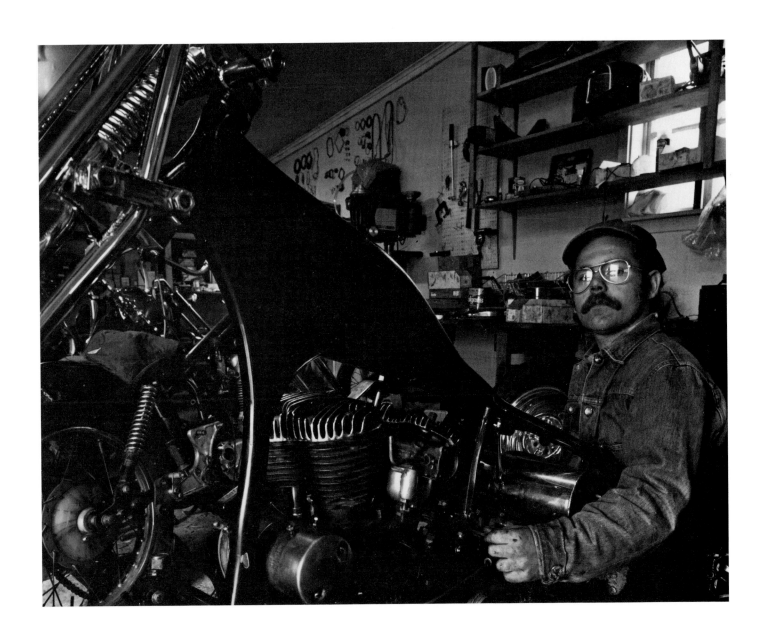

Railroad Redcap

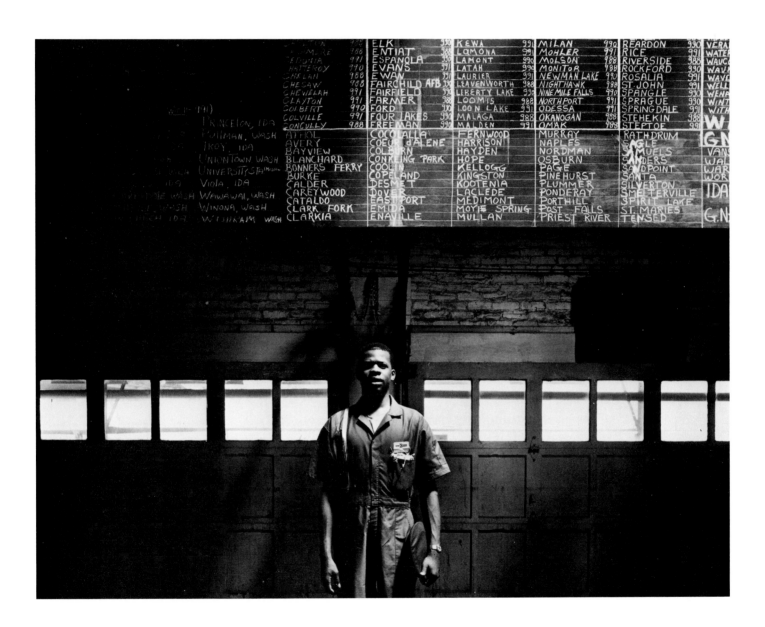

Henry the Sheriff

Henry lived in Shaniko, nearly a ghost town, in Central Oregon. A settlement with a population now of 52, it once claimed 5,000 inhabitants. He was the local character, the town eccentric. He always wore badges, a cop's hat and a cap gun, chewed tobacco which dripped down his chin and made his speech almost incoherent. He remembered all the old gunfights from the town's past. Whether or not he actually saw them or had just heard about them, he was the hero in the incidents he recounted: the outraged man who shot the cheating gambler, or the sheriff who arrested the drunken cowboy who was shooting out the hotel windows.

Henry spent his days sitting on a bench outside the large brick hotel where he lived or wandering up and down the town's only street, waiting to tell his stories to a tourist who stopped for food or gas. He posed for pictures, alone or together with somebody's spouse or child, pointing his pistol at them as if he were an arresting officer. People liked that kind of photograph—a trophy from the boondocks. But Henry always demanded a dollar after the session. The tourist felt either too ashamed or embarrassed not to give it.

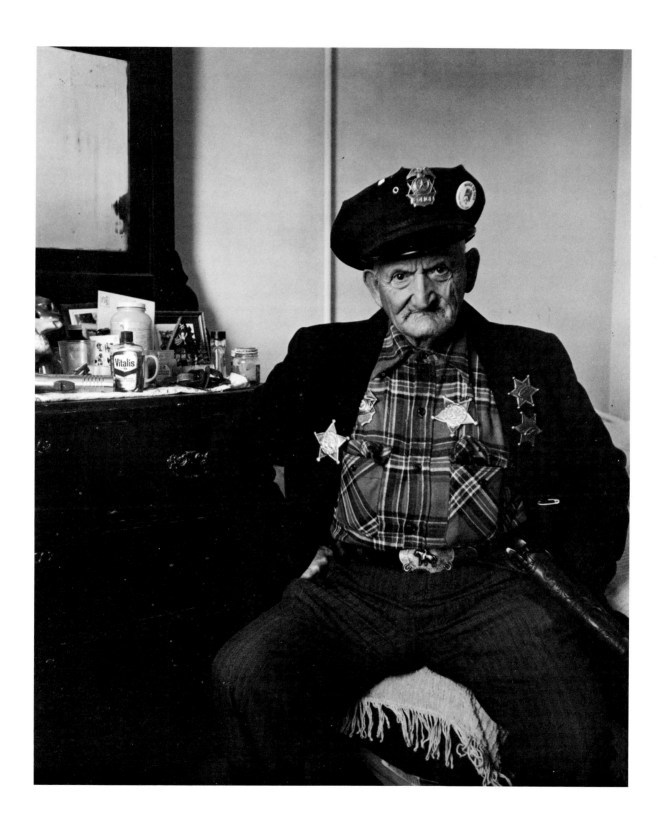

Andrea

She was my wife and is now my best friend.

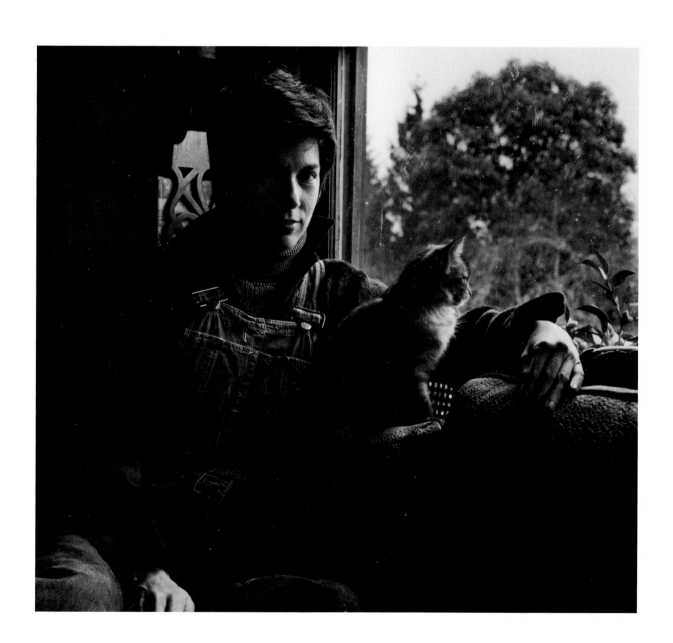

Thelma

In the exclusive side of town, she and her husband had lived in the same tastefully decorated house overlooking Portland for the past forty-five years. A grand piano with sheets of music from the twenties crowded the living room. I was there on assignment from a local magazine to do a portrait, because she was the first Princess of the Rose Festival, a yearly celebration commemorating the advent of spring, which in the Northwest means sun. Spending the afternoon with me, she remembered every detail of the day in 1917 when she was crowned—the parade, the train ride around the state and the banquets. All the memories were in a large photo album: pictures, diary notes and newspaper clippings.

Several months later a Portland museum had a show of my portraits and I sent her an invitation to the opening. She arrived in the same dress and brooch as in the picture and spent the entire evening standing beside her portrait. She posed for photographers and answered questions from curious and admiring guests.

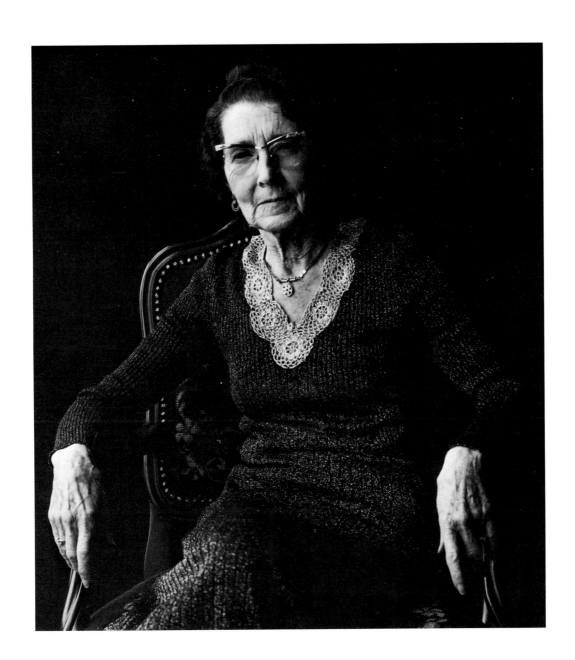

Roxy and Darcelle

They have been a couple for years. Darcelle owns a local bar that caters to the gay crowd on the weekdays but features drag shows on weekends, attended by a predominantly straight clientele. The two men perform in the show. Roxy is notorious for one number in which he wears a tutu and roller skates.

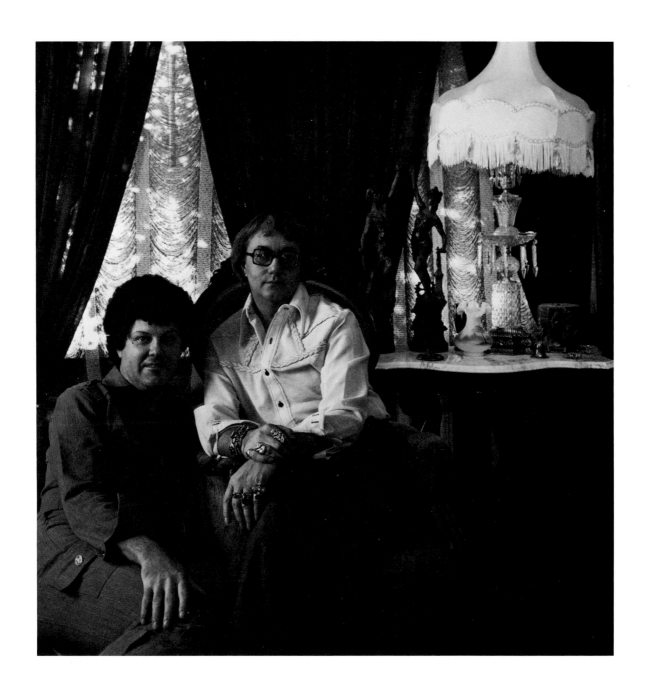

Betsy and Sheri

They are roommates and both attend the community college, Sheri as a teacher and Betsy as a student. The apartment is also shared with Joyboy, Sheri's English sheepdog, and her four doves.

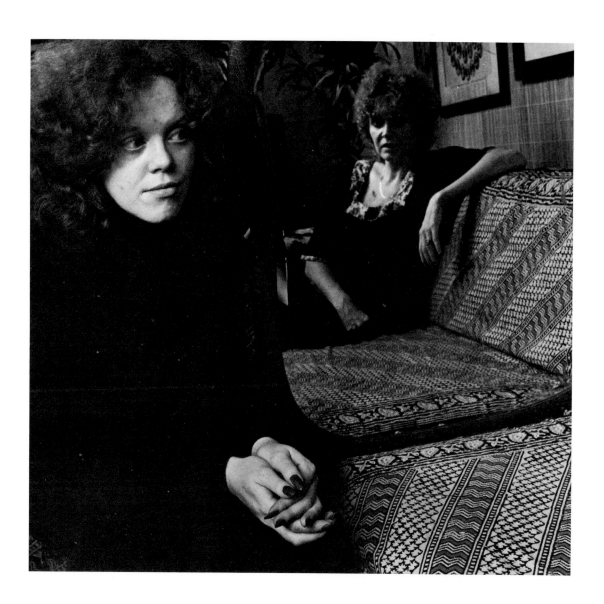

Diana

Strong, gentle, elegant and compassionate. She died of an aneurism to the brain a week after I did this portrait.

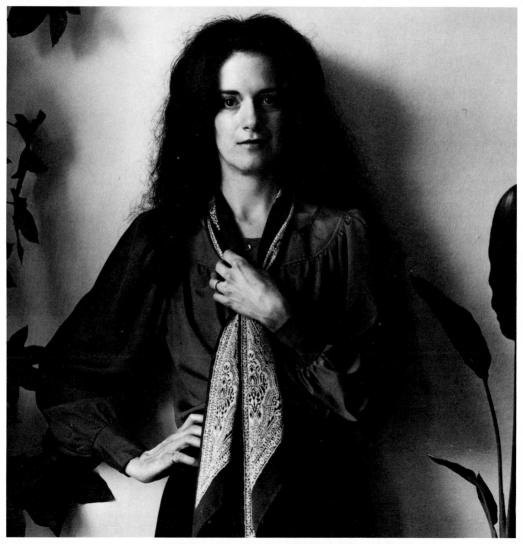

Sara

    A beguiling and affectionate eight-year-old. The only person to consistently beat me at Monopoly.

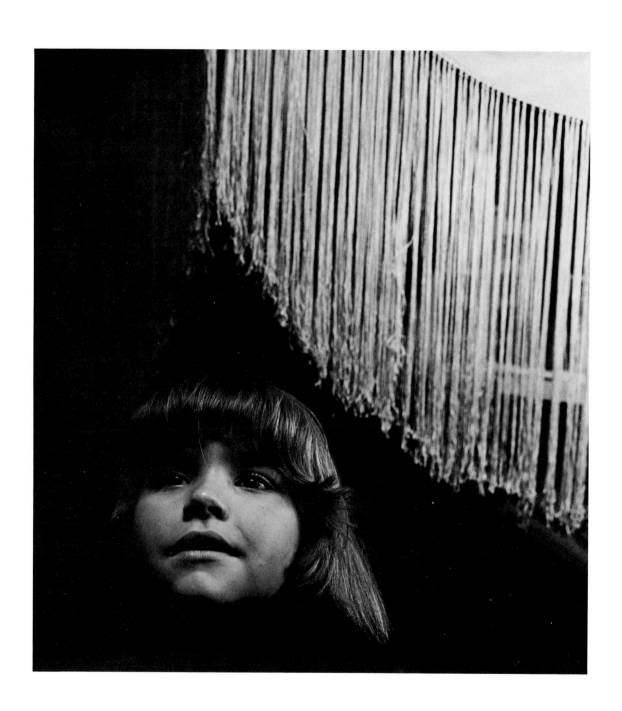

My Sister Ursula

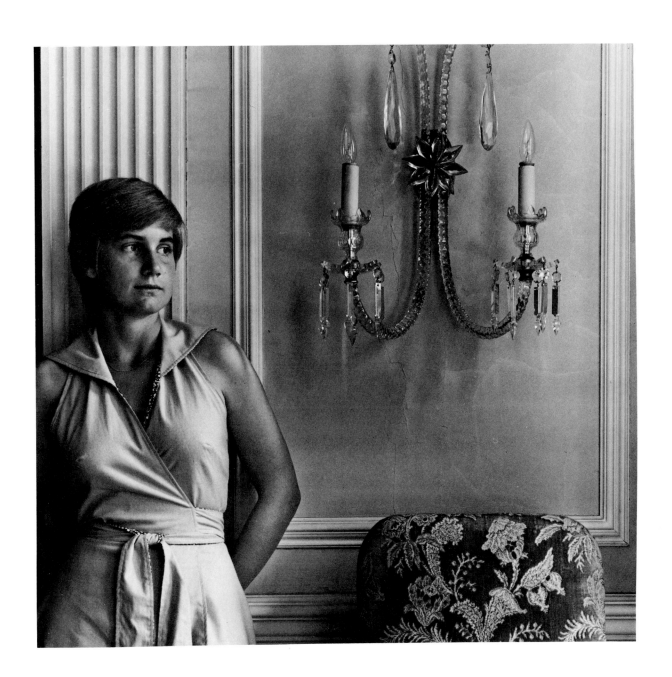

Susan and Claudia

They had recently become friends. They now live on the Oregon Coast. Susan is a woodworker and waitress and Claudia is an actress.

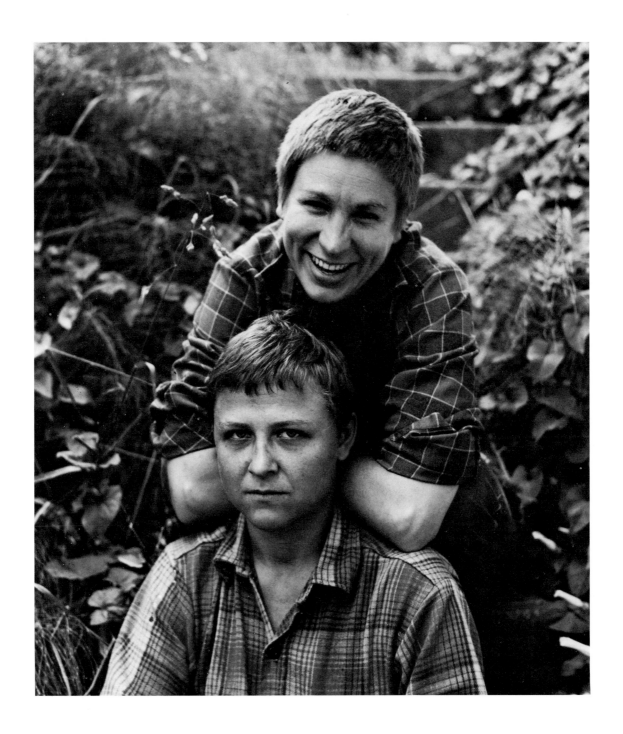

Luke and Addie

Addie's husband, B, is an avid sports fan, especially for Boston-based teams. Just before their first child was born, Luke McKenzie of the Boston Bruins hockey team scored the deciding goal for the championship. Thus, the next day when the baby was born he had a first and middle name. I've known B and Addie for thirteen years, and they are the only couple I know in my age bracket who have been married for eight years with no divorce in sight. Addie is an energetic woman full of humor and mischief. She always reminds me of a sea otter.

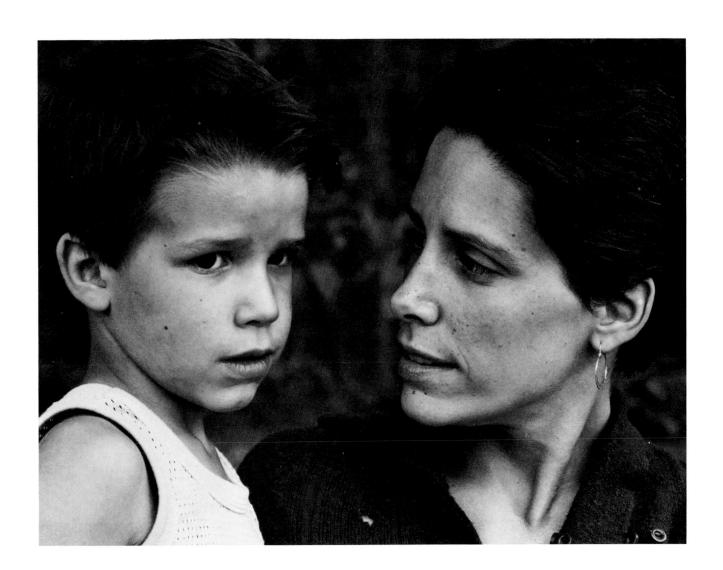

Street Musician

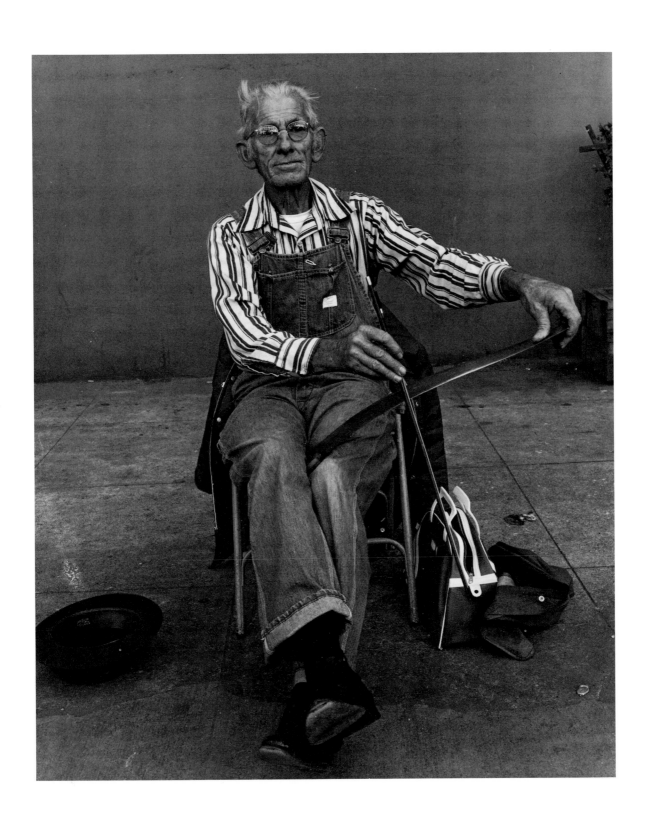

Halloween Party

I was invited to a Halloween party by some friends and, as is my nature, I brought along my camera. I did some individual portraits of people in costume: the Phillip Morris bellhop, Robin Hood, the Statue of Liberty, the Marquis de Sade and an elf. At one point during the session, these friends asked me to do a group shot.

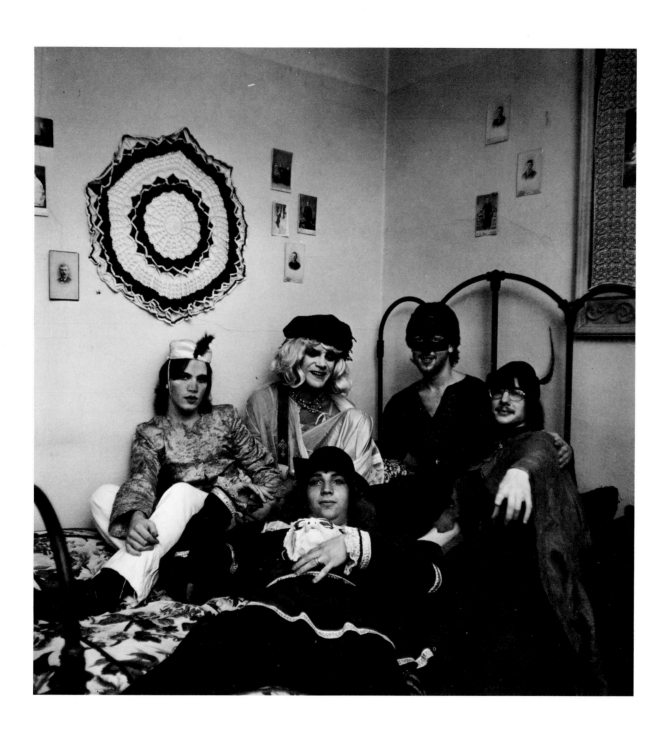

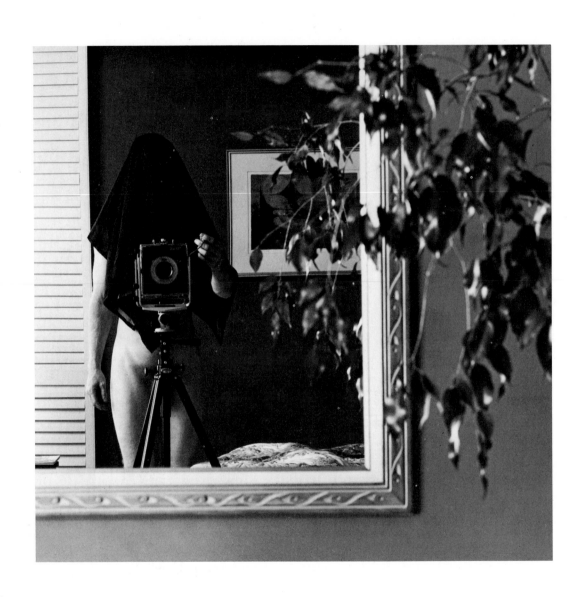